# California Pioneers
## Their Stories, Culture and Cuisine
## 1800 to 1920's

## Elizabeth Cox

Elizabeth Cox
Enjoy!
Dec. 2005

**McKenna Publishing Group**
Indian Wells, California

California Pioneers
Their Stories, Culture and Cuisine
1800 to 1920's

ISBN: 1-932172-14-9
LCCN: 2005920812

Cover design by Leslie Parker
Cover art by Elizabeth Cox

First Edition
10 9 8 7 6 5 4 3 2 1
Printed in the United States of America

Visit us on the Web at: www.mckennapubgrp.com

With love to:

The First String:
Cindy and Shari, Donna and Wendy,
Jon, Kristi, Anthony and Michelle,
Ryan and Leslie.


And to:
Elsie, the other E. Cox.

And:
Mary Egan Martinez

# ACKNOWLEDGEMENTS

With gratitude I would like to thank the following people and organizations for their expertise and help:

Eric Bollinger, Sr. and staff at McKenna Publishing Group.

Christopher Cox, photographer.

JEC Collection.

James Cox, (The beret is picture-perfect).

In addition to the readers' bibliography at the end of this book, my research would not have been successful without the cooperation of the following organizations:

Bancroft Library, University of California, Berkeley, CA.

California Historical Society, San Francisco, CA.

Huntington Library, San Marino, CA.

Smiley Public Library, Redlands, CA.

# CONTENTS

PART THREE: CUSINE
Authentic recipes from California pioneers with tidbits of historical
narrative.

Potato and Wine Salad · Scalloped Tomatoes · Gold Rush Vegetables · Loma Linda Entrée Salad · Crunchy Corned Potatoes · Automobile Picnic Salad · Poetic Salad For A Sunday Gathering

# INTRODUCTION and TRIVIA

In my previous book, *Southern California Miscellany* I concentrated on the southern most region of California. Now, with *California Pioneers* I have turned my attention and broadened my perspective to discovery of some of the lesser known historical stories and anecdotes regarding all of California.

Given a much larger territory to draw from, I have—once again—left no stone unturned in my efforts to unlock backdoor stories from California's most intriguing folk histories. Researching and writing folk history is a passion that transports me back in time to unusual places, affords me the rare opportunity to acquaint myself with personalities from the past, familiarize myself with cultural trends from over a century ago... And exercise a great deal of curiosity when reading between the lines of authentic *antique* recipes—that speak volumes about the way people lived in the pioneering days of early California.

Whether you are new to California or a lifelong resident, whether you are a visitor or California born and raised... I invite you to travel along with me as we cross the threshold of time and experience the folk history, culture and cuisine of California's rip-roaring pioneer legacy from 1800 to 1920... that is *California Pioneers*.

But first, a bit of fun regarding California trivia... Learn from these entries and you'll be sure to stump even the most dedicated California enthusiasts.

**Eureka! You Found the Answer.**

1. The California poppy (*Eschscholiza california*) was designated California's State Flower by the California State Floral Society on December 12, 1890. The process required voting for one of three candidates: Matilija poppy, mariposa lily or the California poppy. Mariposa lily received only three votes, the Matilija poppy garnered zero and a landslide victory went to the California poppy.

In October 1816, scientist Adelbert von Chamisso first described the California poppy as a sparkling yellow-orange wildflower. As a member of an expedition to San Francisco aboard the Russian ship *Rurik*, Chamisso collected specimens for botanical study, which he explained in great detail in his published report of 1820. Chamisso named the bright golden flower for the *Rurik* expedition's doctor—and his close friend—Johann Freidrich Eschsholtz.

The California poppy grows prolifically in nearly every county and is most often in bloom from March through July. In milder climates, the flower continues to blossom into October—such was the case in San Francisco in 1816. Today, one of the largest displays of the California poppy happens annually at the Antelope Valley California Poppy Reserve. Located fifteen miles west on Highway 14 near Lancaster, this State Reserve features over 1700 acres of wildflower extravaganza. But of course, the star of the show is the California poppy.

2. Who's the beautiful woman gracing the official seal of California? It is none other than the Roman goddess, Minerva, identified in Greek mythology as Athena. She is most closely associated with the attributes of virginity, courage in battle and prosperity in agriculture—specifically the olive tree. Athena is the patron to scholars who study the attributes of wisdom gained from prudential justice. And whether she is called Minerva or Athena, she is often depicted clad in armor with a shield and an owl nearby.

3. The California grizzly (*Ursus californicus*) has been extinct in California since 1922, when it was reported the last bear was killed in Tulare County. The grizzly was sanctioned the official California State Animal

in 1953. The close association between grizzlies and Californians dates back over three hundred years to Spanish California when it was estimated over 10,000 bears roamed statewide.

In the early 1800s, grizzly bears were hunted in abundance and prized for their meat, hides and as star competitors in bull-to-bear fighting. The sport was immensely popular and often drew large crowds to bull-bear arenas specially built for these occasions. Many accounts are recorded of bull-to-bear fights in the pueblos of Los Angeles, San Diego and San Francisco.

Feared, respected and coveted by settlers and hunters alike, it is no surprise that the very image of the fiercely independent grizzly bear was selected as the rebel icon for the Bear Flag Revolt in 1846. Fashioning a flag with a star on a broad strip of white fabric, the indomitable spirit of the state supporters in the Sonoma settlement was indelibly and graphically demonstrated when they emblazoned the flag with the image of a lone and defiant grizzly bear. The Bear Flag Revolt quickly became the steppingstone to California statehood. Its iconic flag was refined into the official state flag recognized by all Californians today.

Of all the grizzlies hunted and caught through California's history, by far the most renown is Monarch—so named after the newspaper *San Francisco Examiner*, AKA The Monarch of the Dailies.

In 1889, newspaper magnate William Randolph Hearst hired *San Francisco Examiner* reporter Allan Kelly to capture a live grizzly bear so Hearst could donate it to San Francisco's Golden Gate Park. Kelly and a crew of five men spent six months camped out in Ojai valley of Ventura County before successfully capturing a bear large enough to meet Hearst's requirements.

Dubbed "Monarch" the bear was presented to the Golden Gate Park, which refused delivery. Monarch was sent to nearby Woodward Gardens, and from there, a brief exhibit at San Francisco's Midwinter Fair of 1894. Only when the fair closed did Monarch find a permanent home, when at last, he was welcomed into the Golden Gate Park where a concrete pit was prepared especially for him.

By 1903 Monarch's bachelor lifestyle was beginning to wear thin on his temperament. Hoping to improve his overall welfare, Hearst purchased a bride for Monarch. After several weeks of courtship, the two bears struck an intimate rapport resulting in descendents that are carrying on Monarch's legacy to this day. Monarch died in 1911. Stuffed and preserved, he remains in the protective custody of the California Academy of Science. In his statuary state, Monarch served as artist's model for the grizzly bear icon that graces California's modern day flag.

4. California "Dollars" were not the greenbacks used elsewhere in North America. With the Franciscan missionary expedition to California in the mid-1700s came soldiers and their black Spanish cattle. Rangy and long legged, the first 200-head of cattle were well suited for the diverse Alta California terrain and they thrived on native grasses that profusely covered large expanses of the region's interior. In fact, the cattle did so well that an industry of trading their hides and tallow for goods imported from the eastern seaboard of the United States grew as fast has the cattle herds.

In 1816 a popular trade route for California cattle hides, to and from the east coast, was established between ports in San Francisco and San Pedro. By 1822 nearly forty thousand hides were exported annually. These hides were so valuable a commodity that they became known as California Dollars and California Bank Notes. Dried and baled, California Dollars were traded with Boston sea captains for dried goods ranging from exotic textiles, such as lace and velvet, to custom-made furniture and imported wine. In Boston the hides were turned over to leather manufacturers who bartered top prices and then tailored the rawhides into winter outerwear, gloves and hats.

The era of the California Dollars lasted until the mid 1800s, when railroad extension into the American West ended California's monopoly on hides.

5. Wyatt Earp—icon of the Wild West—spent much of his life in California…notably the period following his legendary shootout at the O.K. Corral in Tombstone, Arizona. After a few years of wandering the

West, Wyatt showed up in San Diego, on the advice of his brother, Virgil, who lived in the San Bernardino-Colton area.

San Diego's boom period of the late 1880s attracted just about every type of entrepreneur imaginable. Wyatt and his wife Josie came into San Diego itchin' to get back into action and the citizens of San Diego liked having the celebrated couple in their society. Wyatt bought into three gambling establishments in San Diego's infamous Gaslamp District. One was on Sixth Street adjacent to the Hotel James; another was on Fourth Street near Horton's Plaza; and the third gambling hall was on E Street, near the intersection of Sixth. So highly regarded was Wyatt that his penchant for keeping a low profile was protected by the city's top business managers. In fact, in San Diego's city directory of 1888, Wyatt Earp is inconspicuously listed as a *capitalist*—a common and plain description for a business operator of that era.

In later years Wyatt and Josie roamed throughout the West, returning to California periodically. They often wintered in the southern California desert, just across the Colorado River from Arizona in the small settlement of Vidal. Today, in the same area, the town of Earp, California recognizes Wyatt's contribution to law enforcement. In Earp the local post office proudly displays a collection of Wyatt Earp memorabilia—and justifiably so. After all, Wyatt Earp was not only a legendary personality of the Old West...he was a United States Marshall. Wyatt Earp died in Los Angeles on January 13, 1929. He is buried near San Francisco.

Now that you have acquainted yourself with a bit of the Golden State's trivia, I invite you to travel further back in time, page by page, as California's fascinating history unfolds.

Elizabeth Cox
San Bernardino Mountains
2005

# CHAPTER ONE
# PERSONALITIES

**Stagecoach Driver Trades Ribbons For Romance**

Delia Haskett could have been the inspiration for artist Charles Dana Gibson's iconic Gibson Girl of the late 1800s. Elegant tresses of upswept dark hair framed Delia's beautiful face. In admiring her portrait an on-looker would never suspect that the ribbons Delia so dearly loved did not adorn her hair. No, indeed—Delia's beloved ribbons were the reins held firmly in her hands as she expertly captained a team of horses. Delia Haskett was the first woman hired as a contracted stagecoach driver to deliver mail in California.

Driving a stagecoach carrying passengers, mail and the much-coveted payroll *treasure boxes* over rutted trails in early California required an intrepid and skilled driver. It was steady work that paid handsomely and men and women alike sought employment with California's few-and-far-between contracted coach lines.  Independently minded from the get-go, it's no wonder young Delia entertained ambitions of someday driving her own team, making a living for herself, and never answering to any man!

When old enough to ride along with her dad on his stage route, Delia pleaded to take the ribbons. Her persistence paid off one day on a routine delivery while accompanying her father.  On the homeward-bound route, her dad placed the reins in her hands. Delia was all of twelve years old. By the time Delia was fourteen she was entrusted on her own with smaller stage runs. Delia's lucky break came in 1876 when she volunteered on a temporary basis to take the Lakeport to-and-from Ukiah route for an ill driver.

*Delia Haskett*

That particular run was a reverse route traversing the rugged terrain of the Cow Mountains, past Blue Lake, through Scotts Valley and on to Lakeport. For passengers it was a three-dollar one-way fare and eight hours of stomach rumbling along bumpy roads. For Delia, it was a daily ninety-mile round-trip adventure she never grew tired of.

Once, on the delivery to Lakeport, as darkness descended, Delia heard shouts and the thunder of hooves drumming down on her. Choosing to wait it out, she positioned her coach in the shelter of trees and hunkered down in anticipation of the worst possible scenario. As the rowdy voices grew louder Delia bit down on her lip, snatched her rifle and prepared to protect her holdings and her life to the bitter end. Alas, much to her relief the thundering crowd of riders turned out to be a noisy group of lost campers riding hard and singing loudly off key. That night Delia made her last stop in the wee hours of the morning after giving the wayward riders directions on how to get home.

Delia Haskett drove stages until she married in 1885. And she hung up her reins not out of necessity, but for love. She traded in her ribbons for romance to become Mrs. Delia Rawson. The Rawsons moved to Los Angeles where Delia continued exercising her self-sufficient ideas—this time in business and real estate. The well-to-do and socially active Delia spent her retirement entertaining friends with stories of her wilder days…When the only ribbons she wanted were the reins of a coach, and romance never stood a chance against a good team of horses!

## Rattlesnake Dick and Gentleman Jack Powers

Among the criminals that vexed Californians in the 1850s were the unwelcome likes of Rattlesnake Dick and Gentleman Jack Powers. Chances are, these two desperadoes never so much as shared a crooked hand of faro, yet, in the files of *wanted* posters they are indelibly linked as two of California's most-wanted bandits.

So often, pirates are associated with seafaring adventures and treasure chests buried on faraway islands. Not so with the tale of Rattlesnake Dick, the self-proclaimed Pirate of the Placers. Up in the gold country of the Sierra foothills, Richard Barter earned the moniker of "Rattlesnake Dick" working as a miner who grew weary of gold seeking and resorted to gold stealing.

From 1856 to 1859, Barter made a nuisance of himself among the honest, working gold camp residents who had the sorry luck of crossing his path, especially in the community of Rattlesnake Bar. In the 1850s Rattlesnake Bar was a rip-roaring gold camp crowded with cabins and the usual trappings of a boomtown, including men with inklings toward making an easy living. Such was the likes of Barter, who earned the name Rattlesnake Dick from this region where he first plied his trade. Roving between Folsom and Rattlesnake Bar, Barter tramped behind miners whom he befriended just long enough to know their worth, and then, when they let their guard down, Barter robbed them blind.

News of wrongdoing traveled like quicksilver throughout gold camps and soon Barter's highwayman ways were too well known for him to continue. So he took a shine to planning a heist that would set him up for life. Barter assembled a motley crew of men—who shared his ambitions in life—to help execute one of the biggest robberies in California history: the holdup of a Yreka mule train laden with 80,000 dollars in gold.

The heist went as planned except for the unwieldy weight of the gold. Since the booty was too heavy to haul in a single raid, Barter carried half the gold out to Trinity Mountain and buried it on a foothill. A posse caught up with the robbers and recovered half the loot. The remaining 40,000 dollars is *still* unclaimed and is buried somewhere on Trinity Mountain protected in death by the Pirate of the Placers: none other than Richard Rattlesnake Dick Barter.

And then there were the dastardly deeds committed by Jack Powers under a sly ruse of gentlemanly behavior. He was a prince of social deceptions and a king of bandits.

By all appearances Powers was known as a proper businessman, sportsman of the highest caliber and a socialite whose name appeared on society's 'A' list. From San Diego to San Francisco, Powers finessed his way into the parlors of California's elite residents, all the while banking on their gullibility to his charm.

Typically, when scamming, Powers weaseled his way into social circles that provided him with insider news of financial investments, cattle sales, property transactions and his favorite topic—the transportation of gold. Once he was privy to such information he spent several days planning a robbery and an elaborate disguise to protect his cover.

As his successes tallied up he grew over confident and careless. Such was the scenario one evening when he sought to waylay a planned target on horseback along El Camino Real near Arroyo Grande. This time, however, his intended victim got the better of Powers and answered the bandit's demands with the business end of a pistol. Powers rode away with a gunshot wound in his leg.

Powers made a feeble attempt to get medical aid and tried desperately to protect his cover by explaining to a doctor that he suffered his injury when he was bucked from a horse and landed on a sharp stick. Not believing Power's story, the good doctor advised him he recognized a gunshot wound when he saw one. Powers hightailed it out of the doc's office and hustled down to Mexico with a posse hot on his trail.

While in Mexico, Powers crossed paths with a former partner named Monet. The two quarreled with a pair of firearms and according to folk history, ended up shooting each other to death. When the posse arrived the next day they discovered wild hogs devouring all that remained of Gentleman Jack Powers and the motley Monet.

### The State's First School Teacher

On a miserable rainy day in December of 1846, California's first state school was established through the courageous efforts of Olive Mann Isbell—pioneer, wife, nurse and teacher.

Olive and her husband, Dr. Isaac "Chauncey" Isbell were married in Ohio in 1844. Shortly after, they moved to Warren County, Illinois, where Chauncey practiced medicine for two years, then they headed west with California as their destination. The Isbells left Springfield in April of 1846 under the guidance of wagon master Joseph Aram. Three additional wagon trains joined the Isbells at Fort Laramie where they learned of the outbreak of the Mexican-American War. Contending with the news that California was a hotspot for battles, the wagon train families had to make the crucial decision to continue or stay put. Around a campfire the debate continued well into the darkness until Olive stood and with quiet determination proclaimed, "I started for California and I want to go on." A few families turned back. Others rallied by Olive's unwavering sense of destination and voted to continue.

The pioneers reached the Sierra Nevada Mountains and were met by

John Fremont near the Bear River Pass. From there Fremont escorted them safely to Sutter's Fort, and then on to Mission Santa Clara de Asis, where, at long last, on October 16, 1846, after an arduous six-month journey, they unpacked and set up homesteading.

Many of the pioneers arrived in California ill from "immigrant fever." For Olive, who had honed nursing skills helping her husband, the days were long and bone-weary as she nursed dozens of men, women and children, including her husband who had fallen ill on the journey. And, although Olive had her hands full, she remained undaunted as, on a daily basis, she administered over a hundred doses of medicine from Chauncey's supplies. Difficult as the days were, the pioneers' resolve was tested to an even greater degree that December as Mexican soldiers stormed the area.

Barricaded within the meager walls of Mission Santa Clara, Olive could never have imagined the horrors she experienced. The numbers of the sick and dying escalated day by day. As medicine became scarce, it seemed that everywhere Olive turned she was met with the stare of illness or the terror of the attack that was raging outside the mission's walls. Indeed, life as it was, seemed far from the promise the pioneers had held so strongly to on their journey westward.

It was the children that Olive's concern turned to in every spare minute she could manage. Hoping she could bring some sense of normalcy to their chaotic existence, Olive began teaching lessons in a darkened room of no more than fifteen square feet. With the clamor of rain beating down over the thunder of gunshots, Olive gathered together the mission's twenty-five children and using the earthen floor as a writing board and a stick for her chalk, she lovingly took the children under her wing and eased their fears with ordinary lessons in arithmetic and reading.

The siege lasted until January first when the American army arrived from Yerba Buena (San Francisco) with artillery and fresh supplies of medicine. After recovering from the nightmare, the families strengthened their resolve and remained dedicated to carving out a future in California.

In early March, Chauncey—now fully recovered—and Olive moved to Monterey. On their fist night in the city, Thomas Larkin, United States Consul, acting on behalf of Monterey's founders, asked Olive to set up the town's school. After hearing of her heroic deeds at Mission Santa Clara, Monterey residents were forthright and dearly determined in their choice of Olive Isbell as the person to establish and teach what they deemed as the state's first school.

Olive began the school in a room upstairs from the town's jail with only a few pencils and paper. The lessons came from Olive's experience, which was just fine by her students.... all two of them. Within a few months student enrollment increased and by then the Isbells were ready to move on to French Camp (Stockton). Olive turned over her classroom to the town's volunteer society.

By the mid 1800s the Isbells had become financially set and chose to travel the world. Yet, wherever they went, Olive carried with her the fond memories of her pioneering days as California's "first" teacher. Olive and Chauncey returned to California and spent their retirement years in Santa Paula, where Olive died on March 25, 1899.

## Sagacious Number Seven

"Never too busy to stand feet apart and hands in the old-fashioned top-pockets of his gray trousers, listening to his office-seeking constituents," is how journalist Fredrick Collins described Governor Friend Richardson in a 1924 interview.

A homespun man with Quaker values, Richardson hadn't won the governor's seat easily. Any witness, friend or foe, will testify he did it the old-fashioned way—he earned it. By the era's standards, Richardson was a rogue Republican whose politicking strategy was a preference for engaging in neighborly chats rather than attend political gatherings.

Campaigning on the platform that he was a man of the people, Richardson went so far as to say, "The best way to get elected is to keep away from politicians." And keep away he did. Richardson positioned himself behind the wheel of his Number Seven automobile and called the open road his campaign trail.

To be sure, he wasn't afraid to listen first hand to Californians' opinions. It was a common sight to see his Number Seven parked off the roadside, with nary an office building in view, chatting it up with local residents he just happen to come upon. After his first few motoring trips, Richardson himself was dubbed as "Number Seven" by his public, which was just about everyone, regardless of their political leanings.

By nature he was a man of the people, by profession he was a newspaper journalist, editor and publisher. Richardson grew up in San Bernardino, where as a young man he had a keen editorial eye and took on the publishing task of the town's newspaper. After ten years of success in the newspaper business he moved to Berkeley. In the politically charged environment of Berkeley he honed his diplomatic skills and thereby took the first step that would lead to the Governor's mansion.

In 1923 the Democratic Party paid him little attention and dismissed him as no more than an accidental candidate for the Republicans' so-called Progressive Agenda. To the Democrats' chagrin, Californians did notice Richardson. So much so, they elected him governor!

*Governor Friend Richardson*

After winning the election—without the help of politicians from either side—Richardson went on to manage the state without political influence. His ethical sense of independence was exceptionally demonstrated when he appointed judges. Not the least influenced about a candidate's political standing, Richardson chose instead to conduct a plebiscite among lawyers in the community and subsequently appointed the man with the highest regard among his peers.

Richardson's non-political appointments were a bitter bite for his fellow politicians to swallow. All the same, to the general public, good old-fashioned Number Seven's mode of operation proved that he wasn't just a man of his word, but a politician true to his name—Friend Richardson was Californians' pal.

## Lola Montez, Irish Dancer

Maria Dolores Eliza Rosanna Gilbert came of age in a world that treasured performing arts as a cultural necessity. She took to heart those values and dared society with her own impassioned interpretation of dance.

Maria, known to the world as Lola Montez, was reportedly born in Limerick, Ireland, in 1818. Lola was known as a person with a colorful imagination who, on more than one occasion, would spin fanciful tales about her heritage, not the least of which was a story that she had been kidnapped by gypsies when she was a young girl. But every so often she would let slip with the *truth* that she was actually the only child of an Irish military officer and a Spanish mother.

Out of concern for her daughter's future, Lola's mother encouraged her to marry a prominent judge who was smitten with Lola's beauty, tolerant of her creative ways and flattered by her interest. The hitch, of course, was that Lola, all of eighteen years of age, would marry a man eighty years old! Lola wanted nothing to do with the arranged marriage and in rebuttal, opted to elope with a dashing and young military officer. She did just that and the two lovebirds sailed off to India.

Exotic India, with its myriad tapestries of foreign cultures and social practices enchanted Lola. So much so that her marriage looked dull by comparison so she entertained herself with the study of dance and dreamed of fame on the stage. It was at about this stage in her life that she assumed the name of Lola Montez... A name far better suited to her aspirations and self-image as a femme fatale.

Lola Montez did achieve her dream and garnered quite a few admirers on her climb up the ladder of success. She was romantically linked to famous musician Franz Liszt as well as adventure novelist, Alexander Dumas. It was claimed in well-circulated rumors of the era that Lola cost Ludwig I of Bavaria his throne. After conquering Europe, Lola set sail for America. New Yorkers were thrilled with her and she captivated New Orleans' society. She then set her sights on San Francisco.

In the city by the bay, she performed her world-famous *Spider Dance* to astounded audiences who gasped at her skimpy and revealing costume. Daringly, Lola flaunted flesh-tinted tights as she squirmed across the stage portraying a woman with dozens of spiders caught in her skirt. She would wiggle the clinging insects free and then stomp them to death as they fell to the ground.

San Franciscans didn't know what to make of Lola's frenzied fight with imaginary spiders. After the stage lights dimmed for the night, Lola didn't receive the reviews she had hoped for, and in fact, many other contemporary performers ridiculed her. A popular San Francisco burlesque team known as the Chapmans used Lola's performance as the basis for a series of spoofed acts they called "Lola Montez in Bavaria" and "The Spy-Bear Dancer." The Chapmans, unlike Lola, played to sold-out theatres with audiences clamoring for the best seats. Lola attempted to put the bad press and the Chapmans behind her as she traveled throughout California. Alas, the Chapmans followed closely behind her and made the most out of it.

Eventually, the theater lifestyle wore thin on Lola Montez. She hung up her dancing shoes and tucked away her tights to settle into a little cottage in Grass Valley, where she grew content to enjoy life as it was, with her storied past behind her.

*The Irish Dancer Lola Montez*

# CHAPTER TWO
# UNUSUAL PLACES

**Giant Arrowhead Discovered**

Nestled in the face of the mountain overlooking the city, valley and county named San Bernardino, State Historical Landmark 977 is simply named "The Arrowhead."

Measuring a giant 1,360 feet long by an expansive 450 feet wide, The Arrowhead points downward to the famous hot and cold water springs which bear its name. Once believed to have been carved by Indians from the mountain side to mark the location of hot springs regarded as healing waters, recent geological studies confirm the arrowhead shaped landmark is a natural phenomenon.

Catholic Padre Francisco Dumetz penned The Arrowhead's first recorded history in 1810. Dumetz was sent to the valley of the arrowhead, from the San Gabriel Mission, to establish an outpost. He named the valley in honor of the feast day of May 20 for Saint Bernardino of Siena. Later, the name was anglicized to *San Bernardino*. Awed by the landmark's natural grandeur, Padre Dumetz built his mission in the direction the arrow pointed to, in the heart of the valley, under the sentry of the landmark and mountains.

Throughout the history of San Bernardino, The Arrowhead has remained a landmark destination for Indians, pioneers and travelers looking for a restful retreat. In the wake of the mission era, and in the founding of the great *rancheros*, Spanish settlers found their way to the valley by using The Arrowhead as their guide mark. Seen from as far away as thirty miles, the landmark kept seekers on a straight arrow path to San Bernardino.

When Mormon pioneers from Utah came to the region in 1851, they looked toward The Arrowhead as the "Ace of Spades." Trailblazer Kit Carson knew of the landmark and of the thirst-quenching relief its mountain springs offered a weary scout. In 1857, adventurer David Noble Smith discovered the therapeutic properties of the Hot Springs as well as the healthful purity of the cold spring's drinking water. Enthralled with his find, Smith built the first health spa retreat. Then, in 1885, the first in a long legacy of health resort hotels was established with the moniker: Arrowhead Springs Hotel.

In 1894, one word described the landmark's renowned presence: WATER.

Chosen as the brand name for water distilled and bottled from the hotel's basement springs—Arrowhead Mountain Spring Water—was marketed to the masses seeking the healthful benefits of drinking pure mountain spring water. By 1900, The Arrowhead was utilized in advertisement as an iconic logo for enterprises throughout the region and in identification for San Bernardino City and County businesses.

Today, the landmark has a shared ownership, ninety percent of which is under the auspice of the United States Forest Service, with the lower ten percent owned by an historic private hotel facility located on the original grounds of David Noble Smith's health retreat. The springs continue to produce thirst-quenching water and relaxing hot springs. A survivor of earthquakes, erosions and wildfires, The Arrowhead is still distinctly visible and remains the guide mark to the San Bernardino National Forest via Highway 18, the scenic Rim of the World byway.

### The Demise of Deadman's Island

In 1840, Henry Dana described Deadman's Island as the only thing in California from which he could extract anything like poetry. Only 800 feet long, 250 feet wide, and 60 feet high, it's a stretch of a definition to call the object of Dana's admiration an island. Nonetheless, to Californians, an island it was.

Located in San Pedro's inner harbor opposite Timmis Point,

Deadman's Island served the living as well as the departed. As an isolated sanctuary of land, just a few miles off shore, the island was both a sentinel to harbor traffic and a city of the dead. Not surprisingly, the chronicles of Deadman's Island are rich with folklore. Supposedly, the island earned its eerie name because it was the final destination assigned to disease-ridden mates from Spanish pirate ships. And while the romantic notions of pirate lore cannot be denied or proven, there is one thread of truth woven into the tapestry of the isle's history.

Sepulchral use of the small cay is traced back to 1810 when a handful of fishermen sought to rest a spell on the island's top point. Much to their dismay, they had to share their view with the remains of a poor soul who perished from exposure. The fishermen kindheartedly laid the body to rest and, in doing so, initialized Deadman's Island as a repository for the dead.

The Island continued in the role of humble servant to the deceased of Los Angeles. During the Battle of Dominguez in 1846, as noted in the writings of Lt. Robert C. Duvall, several soldiers were buried there along with six seamen from the ship *Savannah*. And... aside from being the final residence to pirates, fishermen, sailors and soldiers, Deadman's Island is rumored to be the burial ground of Black Hawk, the last male Indian from San Nicholas Island. As for the female population... Interred in 1858, a sea captain's wife from the ship *Laura Birch* is believed to be the only woman ever laid to rest on the island.

How many people were buried on Deadman's Island? No one shall ever know. In 1928 the island's demise was signed, sealed and delivered in a contract awarded to the United Dredging Company of Los Angeles. On June 1, 1929, the San Pedro *News Pilot* reported that with the final blast of black powder fired, the ocean swallowed the last remaining evidence of what was Deadman's Island. How many souls were laid to rest on Deadman's Island? The answer is locked in the depths of San Pedro Bay, where watery graves harbor the remains of the departed and the ocean waters will never tell.

### Rush to Randsburg

Less than an hour's drive north of Palmdale, nestled at the foot of the Rand Ledges is the historic settlement of Randsburg. Today's Randsburg has a quaint population of a few hundred townsfolk. But a century ago, this somnolent town was one of California's biggest, little gold mining camps.

The rush to Randsburg began, unlikely enough, in the autumn of 1894, when Los Angeles newspaper reporter F. M. Moores caught wind of stirrings at the Goler placer mines. Moores trekked into the desert to see what the hoopla was about. Once there Moores fell victim to the lure of gold and he surrendered his aspirations for journalism in favor of a pick-an'-shovel lifestyle.

His days turned into weeks of laboring through triple-digit heat waves, hellish grit-filled sand storms and meager meals of stale bread and beans. Yet, nothing deterred Moores and in his resolve to find gold in the sun-scorched Mojave landscape he found a kindred spirit in fellow prospector, C. A. Burcham. Prospecting daily from dawn to starlight, the partners were about to toss away their shovels one evening in October when they found themselves low on water, out of food, and a day's journey from the nearest sign of civilization. Addressing a desolate canyon as home for the night, the men respectfully contemplated a change in their lives.

Low and behold! While foraging for breakfast the next morning Moores and Burcham spied a protruding rock ledge that begged confrontation with a pick hammer. Burcham hacked off a fistful of rock, and gazed in disbelief at what it revealed. Jagged pinpoints of gold mocked the morning light! Hunger pains were forgotten in the rush of adrenalin as the partners fervently set to shoveling out the gold-laden ore. By the first week in February in 1896, Moores and Burcham shipped to San Francisco over 58,000 dollars in ore. With that first load, news of the strike spread like wildfire over dry prairie grass. The rush to Randsburg was on!

Seemingly overnight throngs of gold seekers and camp followers invaded Randsburg. Within three months the quiet town turned from a bend in the road into a rip-roaring mining town. Where dust devils once danced stood four hotels, twenty-four saloons, a host of sporting establishments and one elegant dance hall recruited from San Francisco to serve double duty as a land claim office by day. By spring of 1897 Randsburg was in its full glory as its population swelled to over five thousand as ore was assayed at the rate of 3,000 dollars per raw ton.

Alas, Randsburg's glory days were numbered after its mines ran dry. As strains of jazz ordained the roar of the 1920s, the town was quieted to a hush while the last traces of gold, silver and tungsten were stripped from its hillsides. Randsburg was forsaken and left to bite the dust of the mercurial Mojave Desert.

Today, Randburg has survived by the sheer will of its residents' determination to keep alive the spirit of their Wild West era by operating a general store and antique shops in restored 19th century buildings. Stepping into one of these old shops is to cross the threshold of time. Listen closely and you will hear the echoes of another era...voices from the bygone days of Randsburg's rush to glory.

*Randsburg today*

**Dragon Island's Lighthouse**

In 1792, intrepid seafaring explorer George Vancouver was approaching the northern-most coast of California when he spied an amazing site—a small rocky island that appeared to be spouting smoke much like the fiery breath of a giant dragon. Vancouver dubbed his discovery "Dragon Island". In later years, Vancouver's dragon was renamed St. George Reef—a deadly island tip of a submerged volcanic mountain located six miles off California's coast in Del Norte County.

The smoking phenomenon Vancouver observed is apparent in stormy weather as racing winds and thrashing waves crash upon the island's rocky ledges, creating a thick hurling fog that conceals the dangers lurking below. Like an iceberg, Dragon Island's shape spreads out underneath the ocean surface. Its geological nature has been the cause of shipwrecks when vessels sailed too close and were ripped apart by the dragon's saw tooth shoulders.

Such was the tragedy of the passenger ship *Brother Jonathan* in 1865. After taking off from San Francisco Bay, the ship hit rough seas and the captain thought best to head north to the safety of Crescent Harbor. On the approach the captain attempted to navigate through St. George Reef. Alas, the weather had taken a turn for the worse and the dragon was up to its old tricks. The ship never stood a chance against the dragon's smoke; it hit the outer circle of the island's ragged edge and was shorn to pieces. Nearly two hundred people drowned as they jumped ship and were swallowed by the turbulent sea.

The *Brother Jonathan* tragedy prompted the construction of a lighthouse on Dragon Island. Considered one of the greatest lighthouses in the nation, building it also earned the facility the distinction of being one of the most costly maritime endeavors. Construction began in 1882 to the tune of 100,000 dollars granted by Congress. By the time the lighthouse flagged its first signal in 1892 the total tab came in at 704,633 dollars! Officially named the St. George Lighthouse, the facility sits on a concrete pier 70 feet high, featuring a tower 134 feet tall made from 1339 granite blocks.

The arduous ten-year span of construction is but a hint of the challenges encountered by lighthouse builder George Ballantyne. Building the facility required housing a crew in a makeshift barracks on board the lightship, *La Ninfa*. In its initial use, the single mooring the barrack-ship was tethered to proved futile when a storm caught the crew off guard and the tether broke. The *La Ninfa* drifted out to sea and was discovered about a week later, after which a hefty anchoring line was attached to secure the floating barracks. That wasn't the only challenge Ballantyne surmounted. Faced with the perplexing problem of offloading supplies onto the island, he devised a ship-to-island aerial tramway to deposit workers and supplies on the island.

True to the desolate nature of the lighthouse's location, the facility saw more than the usual number of keepers. Faced with an overwhelmingly lonely existence, over eighty men took leave of their assignments from 1891 to 1930. Highlights in journals describing lighthouse keepers' difficulties include:

1918-1937: George Roux was head keeper. During this time, he and his crew experienced the worst weather on record in a continuous span lasting 59 days. During the ordeal the men sank into a depression so deep that not a one would so much as utter a word to the other. Once the weather broke and a supply ship made its delivery, the men's demeanor slowly normalized.

1892-1939: Log records show that the isolation was at a peak…only five visitors per year made the trip out to the island. And these included the regular round of inspectors!

1951: The worst lighthouse tragedy in California history took the lives of three Coast Guardsmen after waves capsized their boat when returning to shore.

1952: Worst winter on record as 160-foot waves crash over the lighthouse. One keeper suffers a mental and physical breakdown and is retired from service.

Truly unique in maritime history, Saint George Island Lighthouse was decommissioned in 1975. After many years of lobbying to preserve the facility, the St. George Reef Preservation Society received jurisdiction from the U.S. Government in 1996. Thanks to their efforts, this amazing facility remains an active reminder of California's seafaring legacy.

## The Thunder of Tahquitz

Exercising his dominance over the alpine sky, Tahquitz roars, and his thunder clamors through the peaceful forest. Sequestered in his mountain prison, Tahquitz stands sentinel over Idyllwild—a relentless reminder to all, that he alone, is the god of mountain legends. The Cahuilla Indians have passed this oral history from one generation to the next since time immortal in the San Jacinto Mountains near Palm Springs. Cahuilla history recounts the tale of the brash warrior who was born from the rugged land of San Jacinto to become chief.

In the beginning, before time was measured and days were recorded on paper, all people of Cahuilla lived in peace with each other and in harmony with nature under the leadership of Tahquitz. After several seasons of prosperity, Tahquitz's desire for power overcame him and in his greed he demanded more than his share of the tribe's offerings. Still, his people honored him and continued to meet his demands.

Then the season of sorrow came. Cahuilla children vanished, one by one. Mothers wept as fathers banded together to search for their missing children. One father followed his child's footprints to the home of Tahquitz. When the chief admonished the father for his suspicions, the two fought. In their struggle a large basket was upset. As the basket turned over, decapitated heads of all the missing children rolled out onto the barren floor.

The enraged father overpowered Tahquitz and dragged him to the tribal center to burn at the stake. As the mighty chief perished in fire he manifested his being into a ball of smoke, escaping upward toward the mountain's peak of San Jacinto.

Cahuilla men followed the spiraling smoke and reached the peak in time to see Tahquitz take refuge inside a cave. Quickly, the men gathered together and in brute force lodged a huge bolder across the cave's opening—sealing the fate of Tahquitz for all eternity. Vowing thunder and lightening as his revenge, Tahquitz continues to protest to this very day.

Of late, Tahquitz has met his nemesis, for his thunder cannot drown out the beautiful sounds made by the ISOMATA. Playing to the thunder of Tahquitz, the ISOMATA fills the forest with glorious music

Since 1950, the ISOMATA (Idyllwild School of Music and the Arts) has provided opportunities for students of all ages to study the visual and performing arts at Idyllwild's magnificent alpine forest setting. Besides operating the only independent residential high school for art study in the American West, the school offers courses for children as young as five.

Highlighting all of these extraordinary programs is the summer festival of concerts that range from chamber music, to jazz combos, to symphony orchestras. And much to the displeasure of Tahquitz, it is ISOMATA's musical presentations that have defeated the angry chief's protests—giving Idyllwild a new legacy of sound so sweet to the ears that it has quieted the roar of Tahquitz's thunder.

# CHAPTER THREE
## CRITTERS AND SUCH

### Flea Circus in Orange County

Fourteen-year-old Merle Ramsey awoke to birds singing on a mild late-winter morning in Santa Ana. It was March 5, 1902, the teenager's second day in his new home. Compared to the bone-chilling winter he had left behind in Ohio, Ramsey thought for sure his family had found paradise. Years later, Ramsey chronicled his response: "No snow to wade through or shovel, no horses to feed on frosty mornings or evenings…what a delight!"

Enjoying the mild climate, Ramsey didn't waste a minute investing wholeheartedly in the typical teenage amusements of swimming, fishing and hunting. And while swimming and fishing could be taken at leisure, the boy quickly discovered that hunting was an increasingly time-consuming enterprise. For in the seemingly ideal weather of Orange County there lurked a never-before-encountered definition for *hunting*: ridding one's self and belongings of stubborn fleas!

Californians experienced many types of booms prior to 1900. There had been land booms, agricultural booms, railroad booms… and in the late 1890s, a flea population boom. Vexed by the orneriness of California fleas, Ramsey complained that they were no respecter of persons, clean or dirty, rich or poor. They welcomed everyone. Truly, these were equal-opportunity fleas that made no distinction between calendar seasons and willingly sanctioned their activities upon critter and human alike without preference for soil or linoleum.

Applying dogged determination and methods that seem bizarre by today's standards, Ramsey customarily performed a hunt for fleas. He began each morning with the chore of saturating house and yard with water to deter fleas from propagating in the dry soil required for breeding. All the while, routine daytime activities were performed as people plucked fleas off each other. It was particularly considerate and looked upon as a friendly gesture that in the course of a conversation one would pick a pesky flea off of a friend without interrupting the chat. Neither did nights bring relief. Ramsey recounted a bedtime ritual of stripping beds in search of fleas, noting that if they were flat, you knew they were probably new ones that had come during the day and were waiting for their next meal.

After a while the flea infestation absconded and modern technology stepped in with flea powders, sprays and collars. But for a few seasons, when the flea circus came to town, Orange County was the itchin' and scratchin' capital of California. Years later, Merle Ramsey professed that had he the convenience of buying a flea collar—he gladly would have worn such collars on his own neck, wrists and legs.

## Shooting the Bull on Goat Island

Nestled in the center of San Francisco Bay, Yerba Buena Island has been the home to Indians, pirates, entrepreneurs, the Navy, a lighthouse: and the animals from which the small key's best-loved moniker originated—goats.

Goat Island's goats came to live there in 1836 due to the trading enterprise of Captain Gorham Nye. A clever businessman with a talent for making money on the numerous trading vessels sailing in and out of the busy San Francisco port, Nye recognized the need for fresh meat and dairy products in small compact sizes that sea-bound ships required. Goats, an excellent source of meat and dairy, answered seafarers' nutritional quotas and Nye knew he would not face opposition to raising herds of goats on an island away from the general population. So, as the story goes, Nye set up goat farming on Yerba Buena Island... the ever convenient last stop for out-sailing ships.

As years went by and the goat population grew, Nye's business venture caught the attention of traders, including Thomas Dowling who took possession of the property in 1848. Dowling and Nye entered into an amicable agreement in which Nye continued to live on the property and mentored Dowling on the fine art of goat herding. All went well, aside from a few feeble attempts of claim jumping which Dowling's long-barreled shotgun abruptly ended. And, occasionally, Dowling was an impromptu host to inept sailors who either became lost or underestimated the weather and found themselves deposited upon shore of the island. Such was the reason for Dowling to find a means of discouraging uninvited visitors by securing the watchdog attributes of a full-grown bull.

Naturally inclined toward protecting its territory, the bull was given reign over the island and the burly beast's talents worked beautifully at keeping visitors at bay... and in the bay. In fact, so bullish was the animal that it soon became a menace and Dowling was forced to come to terms with his raging bull by forming a hunting party. In order to dispatch the sly creature, who was neck and horns ahead of any human in knowing all the crannies to hide out in, the hunting party split up to cover the island in one fell swoop of hunters' determination.

Six men, armed to the hilt, came across the bull. But before they could take aim, the bull charged, forcing all six men up a tree. Not a bad location to shoot from, if they hadn't dropped their rifles in haste to reach the safety of the tree branches. All they could do was look down in amazement as the bull paraded around the tree, snorting and stomping their weapons into bits and pieces.

The men were rescued near dusk when the rest of the party caught up with the bull and lassoed it into submission. Corralled, Dowling's bull was shot and barbequed the next evening. Nonetheless, in the end, the bull was not without his glory... Immortalized in local folklore by this anonymously-penned ditty:

"On Goat Island's secret shore
Many the hours we've whiled away
Listening to the breaker's roar,
Which haunts the beach, both night and day
When we landed on the isle,
Dowling met us with a smile,
And his bull gave us a roar
As we left Goat Island's shore."

## Chickens, Cows and Gophers Fool Gold Miners

Of all the stories panned from California's gold camps of the 1850s, the true accounts of miners examining chickens, cows and gophers for gold are among the most bizarre.

Chickens—a miner's favorite Sunday dinner—were ever present in camps and were given free range to peck out a living. Well aware that chickens persistently gleaned the ground in and around camps, cooks always searched a chicken's gizzard before cooking the bird into the day's blue-plate special. On one occasion at the Diamond Springs camp in 1856, a single chicken gizzard rendered $12.80 in granular size gold nuggets!

Then, there was the miner's standard livestock of cows. Every camp had at least one milking cow and some miners had their own pet bovine. Cows were allowed to graze freely and opportunistically. The problem was that meandering bovines had an uncanny appetite for leather goods. Such was the case in Yreka one warm afternoon in 1855 when a miner shed his coat to gather firewood. Tossing his jacket over a tree stump, he paid no heed to a lone wandering cow that moseyed over to keep him company. The miner busied himself gathering firewood and only gave the cow attention when he noticed it plucking his buckskin bag of gold dust from his jacket pocket. Dropping his firewood bundle he ran toward the cow just in time to see her swallow his bag of gold. The horrified miner corralled the cow in hope she would *deposit* his gold. Alas, she kept the gold. And after ten days, faced with no other alternative, he killed the cow, retrieved his 500 dollars in gold dust from her belly and then invited his fellow miners to join him in a barbequed beef dinner.

By far, the most extraordinary incident involving gold-snatching critters happened around the same time along the Stanislaus River at a gold camp near Carson Creek.

An old-timer, who kept to himself, and was viewed as a recluse by fellow miners, got the entire camp in an uproar one morning when he went into hysterics claiming all his gold had been stolen during the night.

Sympathetic to his loss and eager to catch the low-down thief, all the miners went to his aid. At the old-timer's tent a crowd of men gathered around the gaping whole in the earth where he had buried his treasure of nuggets. Careful inspection with a shovel led to the discovery of a gopher hole intersecting the cavity. They followed the gopher's tunnel for twelve feet, unearthing a deeper antechamber that branched off in several directions and in turn, each branch led to a den of compartments. Much to the men's astonishment, they found all the compartments intricately paved in gold nuggets, securely imbedded into the walls and floor—every bit as neatly inlayed, as one would for a brick hearth in a fine mansion. And regardless of size, not a single pebble of gold was left strewn about or deposited outside the dens.

The men handpicked all the nuggets and after weighing the gold, not a single ounce was missing. However, the same cannot be said for the thief. The gold-snatching gopher of Stanislaus was never caught.


**Chino's Belled Eagle**

In 1889 P.D. Green, justice of the peace in Tehachapi, had two eagles. As the story goes (and depending on who is telling the story), Green either captured or found them. After two years of being caged, the eagles got restless looking at life from behind bars and began to exhibit a decidedly negative attitude toward their owner. In self-defense of his pets' talons and beaks, Green did the right thing—he turned the eagles loose. But before the birds flew the coop, Green collared each eagle with a brass bell, or was it a sheep's bell? (Once again, it depends on which version of the story a person is friendly with). The eagles took to the sky and never looked back on their captivity.

A few months later and a hundred miles south, *vaqueros* hard at work rounding up cattle in the Chino hills were mystified by a cheerful tinkling sound that seemed to fill the air around them. Without a bell, cow or sheep in view...where did the chiming bell-notes come from?

Day after day a merry tune resonated throughout Chino Valley and time and again people were caught unaware by the mirthful ringing. A quick glance in the direction of the jingle-jangle was never enlightening and inevitably resulted in a sore neck. Alas, Chino residents came to accept and appreciate the merrymaking. And so it came to be the Chino's hills were alive with the sound of music!

Exactly how did residents finally unravel the rhyme of the mysterious ringing? For years no one ever gave the slightest notion of associating a soaring eagle with the sound of the bell chimes. Why on earth would they? Sightings of eagles were common in those days, but an eagle wearing a bell...how absurd! As mysteries often do, this one solved itself in due time. After the bell eagle became familiar with the area it would occasionally show itself, often swooping close to the earth giving the onlooker a brief flash of the shiny bell around its neck. Stories circulated about the latest close encounter of the bird kind. The eagle was spotted near a pond, on top of a barn, or perched high in a tree. Each time, the bell was clearly seen around its neck. It was official: Chino had a genuine belled eagle as its unofficial mascot... perhaps the only one ever!

Chino's bell eagle became a local celebrity entitled to special regard. It was generally agreed on that this particular bird would not ever be considered fair game. In a rare agreement between humankind and creature, the belled bird lived out seventeen years of life flying high over Chino. In 1906, the *Chino Champion* newspaper reported the popular mascot's death. Chino's belled eagle was found dead—apparently from natural causes—up in the hills over which it had soared.

# CHAPTER FOUR
# LIFESTYLES

**Reading, Writing and Arithmetic in Early California**

When American pioneers of the 1840s referred to themselves as "emigrants," it wasn't because they came to California from foreign lands—it was because they had journeyed westward into a frontier as vast as the horizon and equally as foreign. At that time the United States drew its boundary at the Missouri River and all territory west of the Missouri was unclaimed wilderness, except for California, which was the northern province of Mexico.

Into the West and ever onward the self-styled emigrants trekked. As the first families settled in California they sought to lay down roots and thereby establish a community united by work, church and school. Work usually came by the lay of the land and church services were easily enough accommodated by the practices of traveling clergy. A community school was another matter. After getting townsfolk together to build a schoolhouse there came the challenging task of hiring a teacher. California's early pioneers quickly discovered that teachers were as scarce as a familiar face in a strange land and the few teachers that could be found rarely had qualifications resembling a formal education.

"Teachers came from all walks of life," recalled gold miner-turned-teacher, Prentice Mulford. When Mulford woke to the reality of northern California's panned out gold fields he tipped his hat in the direction of a schoolmaster's job. Facing the daunting expectation of passing a teacher's accreditation test, he explained, "I expected a searching examination, and trembled. It was years since I had seen a schoolbook. I knew that in geography I was rusty and in math musty." Three school board trustees comprised of a doctor, a miner and a saloonkeeper administered Mulford's exam. With a discerning glance the doctor gave Mulford a long once-over, directed him to sit down and then instructed him to spell *cat*, *hat*, *rat* and *mat*. The nervous candidate swallowed hard, took pen to paper and diligently wrote his response and then handed the exam to the doctor. The three trustees scrutinized Mulford's answers, asked him to standup, shook his hand and presented him with the keys to his new schoolhouse. Mulford sighed in great relief—he had remembered his lessons well.

By his era's standards Prentice Mulford was better educated than many teachers and truth be told, the quality of teaching was so poor in 1859, that Sacramento's school superintendent was forced to admonish teachers for misspelling the name of their state as *Callifornia* and *Calafornia*. With progress there were exceptions. For instance, Los Angeles County's Pomona Unified School District, initially part of the San Jose School District in 1867, struck it rich with the third teacher on their payroll. Irishman Patrick Tonner was not only formally educated in English—he was fluent in Spanish, Latin and Greek. Tonner was given the key to Pomona's first school in a district that by the mid-1880s had an enrollment of 500 students.

Today, California's teachers are among the highest qualified in the U.S. Exacting state education laws require all public school teachers to possess the minimum qualifications of a baccalaureate degree, a teaching credential and receive a qualifying score on the California basic educational skills test, better known as the CBEST. No doubt about it, California schoolmarms and schoolmasters of today earn the highest marks possible for their knowledge of the "3 R's" long before they ever set foot inside a classroom.

## California Scrimshaw

The mystery surrounding the origin of the word *scrimshaw* is as old as the seafaring lifestyle and whale hunting industry from which scrimshaw originated.

It's suspected the word is a phonetic name derived from records kept during the great whaling trade of two centuries ago. Captains' logs revealed variations such as *squinshon, scrinshorne, scrinshander*, and *scrimshank*—an Anglo-Saxon definition meaning *idleness*.

Scrimshaw transitioned from a sailor's craft to a maritime art form during the golden era of whaling in the eighteenth century, when carving and decorating ivory and bone offered distraction and entertainment during the idle hours a sailor encountered at sea. At first, scrimshaw was utilized to decorate practical tools and items such as knife handles, buckles, buttons, and canisters. Fanciful maritime themes were etched into ivory and bone—rendered from whale carcasses—using sharpened tips of knives, nails and the ever-present canvass needles utilized to mend sails.

The craft required a great amount of patience, a steady hand, and a good eye for detail as a sailor carved line drawings into ivory or bone surfaces. Once satisfied with the graphics of his artwork, lampblack, squid ink or India ink was then rubbed into the etched surface to penetrate and fill-in carved lines. Next, the surface was wiped dry and buffed to a satiny sheen, leaving a contrast between the light-colored surface and ink-darkened lines creating a picture.

Scrimshaw was in its heyday in California during the gold rush of the 1850s. Ships bound for San Francisco brought passengers and crew from areas on the east coast, where scrimshaw had already gained an appreciative public as an art form that highlighted the adventures of seafaring men. Having found success in gold mining or any one of the numerous trades that evolved from the era's boom in population and industry, sailors retired their sea legs for homes along California's coastline. They retained scrimshawing as a hobby and found inspiration in using different materials while experimenting with non-maritime themes. From this period, one artist remains an icon of California scrimshaw, namely, Charles Durgin.

Born in Laconia, New Hampshire, Durgin was a cabinetmaker who signed on as a seafaring carpenter at age twenty-one. He spent two years on the whaling ship *Monticello* before returning home in 1865. Spurred by news of financial successes along California's coastline communities, Durgin sailed west and set down roots in San Jose. There he set up shop as a master carver of ornate Victorian furniture and interior architecture.

By the 1870s Durgin was firmly established and quite sought after by homebuilders for his exquisite carvings. In his spare time he kept his hands busy entertaining himself with scrimshaw. Pressed into using new and different materials, he settled upon abalone shells as a canvas for his art.

Durgin's use of abalone was unusual and innovative. No one else was using abalone for scrimshaw, and the shells themselves presented a challenge. The black and red shells didn't take to traditional methods of using ink to highlight etchings. Instead, Durgin used hand tools and foot-powered routers for carving intricate designs using abalone's natural contrasting colors to create detail and depth in depicting Victorian floral designs.

Durgin's scrimshaw art gained recognition right away and is still a valuable collectible. So coveted, it was worth stealing in 2003, when a thief broke into the Whalers Museum at Point Lobos Sate Reserve and stole the entire Durgin collection. Smashing a window, the burglar took all forty-eight pieces—the largest collection of Durgin's scrimshaw art. The collection is priceless and irreplaceable. The only other collection of Durgin's is at the New Bedford Whaling Museum in New England where seven pieces are on display.

Today, scrimshaw has reached new heights of popularity as a practical craft and collectable art form. Processes and methods represent traditional styles and materials, as well as computerized techniques and modern manufactured materials. In lieu of using strictly regulated natural ivory and bone, scrimshaw artists can opt to use a resin "ivory" that faithfully mimics the look and feel of the organic material. Additionally, several materials are recycled. Keys from discarded pianos and organs are re-cut and shaped to provide scrimshaw jewelry and notions. Battered and cracked cue balls from billiard games are transformed into three-dimensional scrimshawed figurines.

And while some artists stick to original methods of etching with hand tools and staining with India ink, others choose electric tools and magnified vision lenses to fashion photographic quality art highlighted by an array of colors derived from paint-infused inks.

As a practical and beautiful craft, scrimshaw flourished in California under the masterful techniques of Charles Durgin. True to Durgin's visionary perspective, contemporary California artists are leaders in providing many of the most unique scrimshaw pieces in today's market.

*7 Tips on Scrimshaw Care*

If you are fortunate enough to have a piece of scrimshaw made from organic material such as ivory or bone, here are a few precautions to follow in caring for it.

1. Ivory and bone are porous substances that are relatively fragile. It's best to protect these pieces from unnecessary handling and movement.

2. Never wear them while bathing or swimming.

3. Avoid overexposure to heat and bright sun.

4. If you wear scrimshaw jewelry, apply makeup, skin oils, hair gels and sprays, and perfumes before putting jewelry on.

5. Don't attempt to clean scrimshaw. However, it is a good idea to moisturize it with a little bit of mineral oil, applied with a soft cloth.

6. Store scrimshaw pieces separately, covered with a soft cloth to prevent scuffing.

7. If you display scrimshaw, do so under a glass case to prevent dust from collecting on it.

## Did The Law Become Lawless in 1853?

In an effort to bring a gang of desperadoes to justice, Governor John Bigler sanctioned a legislative act on May 11, 1853 to establish the California Rangers. Akin in purpose to the legendary Texas Rangers, California Rangers wore the badge of law enforcement and rode with the sole conviction to serve up justice whenever and however they deemed appropriate.

Bigler ordered the Rangers into action for the purpose of capturing or killing a gang of criminals known as the Five Joaquins: Joaquin Botellier, Joaquin Carrillo, Joaquin Murieta, Joaquin Ocomorenia, and Joaquin Valenzuela. From 1850 on, it was generally accepted that these five men were responsible for dozens of cattle raids, robberies and murders up and down California's coastline. Whether they acted individually or in teams, it made no difference to Bigler—he wanted all Five Joaquins brought to justice.

*Joaquin Murieta*
*Popular illustration circulated on wanted posters*

Commanding the Rangers was Captain Harry Love, an ambitious officer who knew that eradication of these desperadoes would hasten advancement of his career. Love vowed to bring the Five Joaquins in dead or alive and ordered his Rangers to vigilantly be on the lookout for suspicious Mexicans. Such was the case in July 1853, when Love's Rangers crossed into Panache Pass in San Benito County and came upon an encampment of several Mexican men.

Using vague descriptions of the wanted criminals, the Rangers hastily identified the men as the notorious Five Joaquins. Exactly who pulled the trigger first is unclear. But, when gunshots quieted and dust cleared, two Mexicans were dead. Using the dead men as evidence, Rangers severed the head of one of the men, and the hand of the other. Supposedly, these were taken back to Monterey and sealed in jars of alcohol for preservation.

The severed head became the legendary pickled head of infamous Joaquin Murieta, and the hand was claimed to belong to the notorious Three-fingered Jack. Albeit, no positive identification was ever made of the head and hand, yet that didn't prevent them from being paraded throughout California in a sideshow display of the powers of law enforcement.

Were the right men captured and killed? Or were the men the Rangers brought to justice that fateful day victims of a rush to judgment? Curiously enough, when the Five Joaquins Act passed into law, Rangers were warned not to jump to conclusions regarding identity due in fact that many law-abiding residents share identical names in accordance with California's Hispanic majority. When absolute identity of a criminal is fundamental to the success of law enforcement, one may only wonder... Did the Rangers turn lawful intentions into lawless actions?

**The Grapes of Wealth**

From its inception California has been a paradise of agricultural wealth. And no crop signifies this importance more so than grapes. The fortuitous combination of climate and soil gave winemaking a propitious start from the very beginning of vineyard culture beginning with the arrival of Franciscan padres in 1770.

Initially, the missionaries planted a small crop of grape cuttings at San Diego and followed them with plantings at Missions San Gabriel, Santa Barbara and San Luis Obispo. San Gabriel's first vineyard numbered three thousand vines and produced grapes for over one hundred years.

In 1857, a colony of German immigrants founded a vintner colony in the city they dubbed Anaheim, a name combined from the Santa *Ana* Valley and the German word meaning home: *heim*. So adamant were the colonists at defending their new home and its crop that they constructed a fence five and a half miles long, built from forty thousand willow poles, each eight feet long; and then dug a moat four feet in depth surrounding the fence. The willow tree poles took root, creating a never-seen-before living barricade of trees marking the property line, as well as providing protection from wayward cattle. Using irrigation water drawn from the Santa Ana River, the Anaheim colony were among the first settlers to put down roots as European vintners.

By the mid-1880s, wine production became the pastime of the rich and fashionable. The trend attracted the likes of Senator Leland Stanford, who spared no expense to build one of the largest vineyards in the state. Stanford owned and operated a wine production that claimed over 3,000 vines on his estate near Mission San Jose. Not to be outdone, Stanford's contemporaries followed on the grape path: Senator James Graham Fair, a 49er and Comstock millionaire, built is winery near Petaluma. Senator George Hearst owned a vineyard in Sonoma County, and E. J. "Lucky" Baldwin grew grapes in Santa Ana near his ranch.

However, the one-up-man-ship that the fashionable gentry amused themselves with could not fill a barrel compared to the serious wine-production business of the Italian-Swiss Agricultural Colony at Asti. Its 1897 vintage crop was so huge that there were not enough barrels in all of California to hold the wine, so a reservoir was carved from solid rock to accommodate the overflowing harvest. To date, the rock reservoir is the largest natural wine tank in the nation, when empty, the giant vat can accommodate a dance floor for two hundred persons!

As California wines won international awards for their excellence, many new wineries opened up throughout the Napa-Sonoma region in California's agricultural heartland and elsewhere as in Temecula and in the Inland Empire at Guasti. During the heyday of wine production in the early 1900s, it was at Guasti—just around the corner from Rancho Cucamonga and immediately adjacent to Ontario International Airport— that California could lay claim to the largest vineyard in the world. To-day, California vineyards not only produce world-famous wines, they are accountable for the grape crop used for raisin production, amounting to seventy-five percent of the nation's raisin production.

*Senator Leland Stanford*

# CHAPTER FIVE
# SOCIETY

**Material Origins**

Open your closet, pull out a dress, blouse or shirt and never give a thought to its material origins—a common-day occurrence in today's modern age. Not so a hundred or more years ago when carefree fabrics such as rayon and polyester didn't exist. For California's pioneers the selection of fabrics from which they could make their apparel was simple, to say the least. Yet, these fabrics are still in use...proof positive we still live in a material world.

To better understand and appreciate the clothing of a century ago, here's a rundown on the heritage of fabrics used then—and now.

CALICO originated in the seaport village of Calicut, in the providence of Madras, India. Calico is the best known and oldest common cotton cloth, which is also quite likely the most colorful. Loved for its tiny flower pattern sprinkled over background colors in every hue of the rainbow, Calico is the fabric most closely associated with the pioneering of America. It was used to make everything from dresses to bonnets. And of course, scraps of calico were sewn to create the stuffed toy beloved by many a pioneering child...the calico cat.

COTTON DUCK is a heavy weight, durable canvas-like cotton popularized in the 1800s' manufacturing of hardware apparel such as duster coats, butcher aprons and was even used as floor coverings painted to resemble oriental rugs. Duck is the Americanized form of the Dutch word *doek,* meaning, "summer wear" and was first used by sailors in the making of sails and duffle bags.

CORDUROY literally means *Cord du roi,* "cords of the king." The name and fabric originated in France when the servants of King Louis were ordered to dress up to par with their royal assignments in napped and ribbed cotton that had the appearance and look of velvet. Thus the royal staff was always set apart and elevated in social stature by the "cords of their king."

DENIM is known best in America as the fabric of blue jeans. The fabric came from Nimes, France and the word is an abbreviation of *de Nimes*, meaning of Nimes. Denim was created to meet the demand of French sailors who needed material durable enough to withstand the wear and tear of saltwater. French weavers dyed the warp direction of the cloth with indigo blue, the only dye that stood the sailor's test of sun and saltwater. However, in order to save on cost of dye, the weavers left the fill direction of the cloth vacant of dye, thus creating the unique white-flecked appearance of denim. Later, during the California Gold Rush of the mid-1800s, tailor Levi Strauss designed overalls to meet the needs of gold miners. Strauss experimented with a variety of fabrics before settling on the use of denim. And from his experiment a California original evolved in the shape of Levi's now-famous 501 shrink-to-fit jeans.

GABARDINE is translated from Spanish to English as *gabardina,* roughly meaning raincoat. True to its origin, rain gear and heavy-duty outerwear is what the material was used for. Today, gabardine comes in many weights and is produced for a variety of apparel including men's suits and women's dresses and skirts.

PAISLEY earned a colorful reputation in the 1960s as the "Flower Power" fabric. Truth be told, paisley's history goes back generations to weavers in Kashmir who rendered the swirling curved leaf pattern cloth from wool gathered from the underbelly of Tibetan goats. In the early 1800s, Scottish travelers to India so admired the pattern that they brought back samples to Scotland where they copied the pattern onto native fabrics. The cloth derives its name from Paisley, Scotland.

PLUSH gets its cuddly name from the French word *peluche*, meaning shaggy. In order to be plush, the nap or pile must be one-eighth inch high or higher, a nap lower than that is considered velvet. The use of plush gained in popularity in the 1800s as the favorite material for crafting teddy bears.

SEERSUCKER is a blister-puckered fabric originating in Persia as *shirushaker*. In adapting it to the Western world the name was simplified to make it easier to pronounce and spell in advertising. Because of the fabric's puckered texture, it allows air to circulate and in the 1800s it was a favorite material to use in summer months for bed sheets as well as apparel.

SUEDE is the French word for *Sweden*. French tailors so admired the smooth velvet-like finish the Swedes gave to leather that they named the fabric for Sweden. In the 1800s, Suede was a coveted material for accessories such has handbags, gloves and vests.

TAFFETA's most remarkable trademark is the rustling sound it creates. This is the fabric most sought after in the making of petticoats. Only the finest petticoats were made of Taffeta and every woman worth a ball gown had to have at least one taffeta petticoat in her wardrobe. A Persian word, *taftah* describes the smooth richly textured surface rendered from silk or a silk and cotton blend. The more cotton in the blend, the softer the taffeta—more silk...more rustling!

WOOL is one of mankind's oldest fabrics and evidence of its use dates back to 4000 BC. Wool was not used in America until Coronado's expedition brought Spanish sheep to use for wool weaving. On the California frontier wool was manufactured into warm garments and bed clothing used in everyday living, as well as desirable trade offerings.

### Snooty Snoods and How To Make One

In the journals of fashion history, Scottish lasses, Southern belles and Old West *senoritas* have shared the romanticized image of tucking their long seductive tresses into veiled pouches called snoods.

The snood's precursor was a medieval caul. A net-like covering woven from gold thread designed to conceal a woman's crowning glory. Medieval women decorated their cauls to display social status. No gemstone, pearl or precious metal bead was exempt from placement on a caul if it served the head-above-shoulders purpose of advertising one's status.

About the same era, Scottish maidens adapted the caul's design and purpose for their own cultural use. In the highlands, lasses wore attractive, yet unadorned, snoods to indicate chastity. Thus, the snood became a symbol of a maiden's availability for matrimony, setting her apart from married women in a village.

In time, the practicality of wearing snoods to contain one's unruly or cumbersome hair surpassed a snood's adornment factor. That is, until the 1860s when women were ready, once again, to wear snoods as fashionable hair accessories. From Southern belles to California senoritas, trend-setting ladies at gala balls and holiday fandangos donned snoods. The snooty snood remained in vogue until Gibson Girls of the 1890s decided to retire them to closets. Once again, snoods were only suitable to wear on chore days in order to keep hair tidy and dust free.

Ah…but the snood came back into fashion during World War II when hat-making fabrics and notions were scarce. What was the fashionable patriotic woman of the 1940s to do? Wear a snood, of course! From silver screen to factory assembly lines, snoods were once again the hair accessories of the moment. One can only wonder…When will snoods return to fashion? HOW ABOUT NOW? Here are two easy methods for making your own snood.

Method A: Use A Purchased Hairnet.

Mesh hairnets can be purchased at drug stores and supermarkets. Choose a color to contrast, or match your hair color, or coordinate with apparel.

MATERTIALS: 1 hairnet, 1 plastic comb or barrette, Sewing or embroidery cord (same color as net), Sewing needle: and a piece of circular shaped cardboard, 12-inch diameter.

DIRECTIONS: Stretch hairnet over cardboard circle. Notice the two places where the hairnet ends were gathered and fastened together. One end will be the top of the snood; the other end forms the pouch pocket that will contain your hair.

Using thread and needle, attach plastic hair comb (use a whip stitch) to the top end of hairnet. You may need to gather up excess net into the comb while whip stitching to create the right amount of pouch/pocket for you hair.

Adorn the snood as you wish. Hide the comb by attaching a bow (sew or glue). Decorate the snood body by sewing on beads, sequins or small silk flowers. Let your imagination be your guide!

Method B: The Old-Fashioned Way.

Not as difficult as you might think. And, the final product is truly authentic looking.

MATERIALS: One 15-inch square piece of snood fabric, such as lace from a tablecloth or curtain or petticoat netting (be creative!). Elastic thread matching the fabric color, One small crochet hook (size 3), One plastic comb, one circular piece of cardboard, (12-inch diameter); and decorative notions.

DIRECTIONS: Using crochet hook, make a slip knot with the elastic thread. Start with a loop on the hook, bring thread over hook and draw through loop on chain. Using this basic crochet method, weave elastic on hook through the holes in the fabric, continuing to "chain" around the outside edges of fabric until you have chained all the way around, creating a pouched 'net.' Using the cardboard circle as a form, stretch the snood over it, bringing the ends together, then slip stitch the ends together and attach the snood top to the comb, as explained in Method A. Decorate as explained in Method A.

### *Vaquero* Style

By the time California became a state, its Hispanic culture had experienced generational decades of clothing adaptation derived from the aristocratic styles of Spain. Foremost in the category of adapting fashion to accommodate form with flare and a style of their own were the *Vaqueros*, descendants of renowned horsemen.

The Spanish colonists were highly skilled manufacturers of leather goods and apparel. In the new world they utilized hides from native animals to satisfy the requirements for making leather *botas*, (boots), *chapareras*, (chaps and leggings), *chaquetas*, (jackets), *chalecos*, (vests), as well as, the wide brimmed hat common to the Southwest called a *sombrero.*

Vaquero style originated from necessity and was born out of creativity with an appreciation for artistic appearances. Rendering leather tanning skills passed from generation to generation as Spanish and Mexican families intermarried and colonized California, each craftsman lent his own stylistic concepts to clothing and accessories. Today, two items in particular have endured in popularity as quintessential *vaquero* fashion: boots and hats.

The first *botas* to make an imprint on California soil were worn by Spanish explorers. Designed as high bucket leather boots attached above the knee by leather ties and tassels, these are the boots that were germane to forming an image of Spain's proud and bold pioneering of exotic lands. These are also the same boots that, because of their comfortable wear and sought-after style, were worn by settlers and adopted by Mexicans who perfected the pointed toe, high-heeled boots into what we now commonly call cowboy boots.

Designed to accommodate the horseback kingdom of the Hispanic rancho lifestyle, the boots provided the perfect foot protection enabling the rider to keep steady in stirrups while maneuvering a horse by the touch of a pointed toe or ridge of a deep heel. Making the most of their artistic flare, Mexican boot makers soon provided the option of individualized style graphically illustrated with fancy stitching over custom dyed leathers.

A *sombrero*, the Mexican hat that so aptly served the purpose of shielding its wearer from the sun's rays, was eventually reinvented into the Old West icon known as the Ten Gallon Hat. Reportedly, this style grew from the proper name of the Mexican hat: "*el sombrero galoneado*," from which *galoneado* became "gallon" and the numeral "ten" was used to symbolize its extra-large size. In Western legend, it is believed that in 1863, the famous J. B. Stetson created his, now famous, "Stetson" cowboy hat based on the functionality and form of the Mexican sombrero.

A *vaquero's* complete riding outfit is a study of fashion serving function in an elegant style unmatched anywhere in the closets of history. The *vaquero's* riding apparel consisted of a *sombrero*, attached with an inch-wide cord; on his upper torso he wore a cloth or leather *chaqueta* decorated with colorful braided embroidery and fancy metal or carved buttons. His pants were *calzoneras*, pantaloon-styled trousers that were slit open on the outside of the leg from ankle to hip, exposing an undergarment of leggings. *Calzoneras* were decorated in a manner to match or highlight the dazzling array of colors displayed on his *chaqueta*. A wide sash drawn tightly around the body to accentuate the torso tied the outfit together. The final image was one of bold color and artistic ingenuity, which is echoed today in the fashion parade of styles epitomized by American Western attire.

## Canned Foods Preserve California's Agricultural Wealth

The next time you open a can of vegetables, fruit or tomato sauce, take a good look inside. There's more inside that can than what meets the eye! Canned foods have been preserving California's agricultural and cuisine history for over a century. The proof isn't just inside the can—it's spelled out on the label in the brand names of Del Monte and Contadina.

The Del Monte brand was initially used in the 1880s to categorize a unique blend of coffee created exclusively for the elegant Hotel Del Monte on the Monterey coast. In 1892, the Oakland-based coffee distributor expanded its product line to include canned peaches. Deemed the cream of the crop, the peaches were crowned with the Del Monte label and successfully marketed to the general public.

Then in 1898, eighteen regional canning companies united to form

California Fruit Canners Association (CFCA). The new conglomerate chose several of the merged brands to market as premium products. Del Monte was one of the brands showcased to represent the CFCA's highest quality.

Del Monte's brand success grew as assorted fruits and vegetables were added to the marketing lineup. And in 1916, the San Francisco-based CFCA consolidated its business strategy by promoting a single brand in an all-out nation-wide campaign—of course, that premier brand was Del Monte. As 1919 turned the corner into 1920, the entire nation was enjoying California's bounty of produce under the brand name of Del Monte.

What do tomatoes and the German blockade of 1914 have to do with California history? Contadina, of course! Contadina—a brand name synonymous with some of the finest tomato products ever canned—is a California original that owes its history to the unlikely circumstances of World War I. As the story goes…

Three immigrant Italian families from White Plains, New York had a successful hometown business producing tomato paste. The family business was going strong up until the German blockade prevented them from purchasing the tomato ingredients they depended on from Italy. In an effort to save their livelihood, the small company relied on locally grown products until they heard about the superior agricultural climate of San Jose, California.

The company relocated to California in 1916 and founded the Bell Canto canning company. Bell Canto's quick success garnered the financial interest of a Chicago wholesale grocery investor. In 1918, the two sides combined to create a new brand—Contadina. But why change the label? After all, Bell Canto was successful in its own right. The answer is in the marketing image.

Desiring a name that would appeal to homemakers, the new company chose Contadina, an Italian word meaning "woman of the fields." A phrase symbolic of the intense care by which Italian women selected only the freshest and finest produce for meal preparation. As one of the first canning companies to appreciate the diversity in American culture, Contadina's woman of the fields evolved to reflect the changes in our society. Today, "fields" speaks directly to the myriad options exercised by contemporary women. Symbolically, Contadina still reflects a woman's excellence in their chosen "lifestyle" field—be it home management, career, recreation, lifelong learning or any combination there of!

# CHAPTER SIX
# LANGUAGE

**Trivia: Straight From a Horse's Mouth**

The evolution of American language has rounded many corners throughout history. Not surprisingly, many favorite phrases reflect our passion for, and dependency on, horses. Good, old-fashioned horse sense has its hooves firmly dug into the landscape of our cultural language. And be it trivia or common sense, the following six phrases reflect truths spoken—straight from the horse's mouth!

**Straight from the horses mouth** is an expression of authority and validity that originated in horse racing circles (possibly in Ireland), stemming from the practice of examining a horse's teeth to confirm true age. Regardless of what truth is alleged to be, if it doesn't come straight from the horse's mouth, don't believe it.

Are you guilty of having kept an impatient person waiting—**to cool their heels**— while you use the passing minutes to your own reward? If so, you are guilty of practicing a tactic that dates back to the seventeenth century. This phrase is a version of the literal "to cool one's hooves," referring to draft horses and their knack for taking advantage of a rest period by lying down. Once down, the big horses were slow to stand up, using every minute to their advantage while keeping impatient trainers waiting.

Once upon a time the United States was abundant with **one-horse towns**, and proud of it! After all, to have a horse in town was a great

65

asset. Ah, but times changed as a keep-up-with-the-Jones's attitude crept into society. By 1855, this quaint saying was considered an insult that described nothing less than a town of poor and limited resources. From New York to California, the phrase was also attached to a person so unsophisticated, that surely, they must have come from a one-horse town.

Whenever something differs from what is generally perceived to be normal, the phrase: **a horse of a different color** or a horse of another color is used to describe the observation. There has been much controversy about this colorful saying. Some historians like to credit William Shakespeare, who used a slightly different version as "a horse of the same color" in explaining a plot for his play, *Twelfth Night*. However, England's beloved bard may have snatched the phrase from a hill in Berkshire, England. The White Horse of Berkshire is a well-defined 375-foot long horse profiled on a chalk hill, which, according to legend, dates back to 871 A.D. or older. Over time, the horse outline would have faded in to dust if not for the work of local residents who ardently kept weeds and debris encroachment from turning their landmark into a horse of a different color.

Whoa…Nellie! Hold onto to your excitement and bide your temper: in other words, cool your heels and **hold your horses!** To hold one's horses means exactly that—keep your horses calm and settle them in. In the American West of the late 1800s this saying described a person who was getting a bit too riled over an exaggerated cause. Often, the phrase was a good-natured reminder that patience wins out over anger as decisions made in haste readily lend themselves to regrets.

Changing direction during a crisis is rarely a wise move. Abraham Lincoln drove home this bit of wisdom when he addressed a delegation for the National Union League in 1864. That league notified Lincoln of their intention to support him in his presidential re-nomination. Of course, the *crisis* was the Civil War and Lincoln wasn't the least bit fooled by any great show of confidence in his leadership. In his address Lincoln said, "I do not allow myself to suppose that either the Convention or the League have concluded to decide that I am either the greatest or the best man for America, but rather they have concluded it is not best to swap horses while crossing the river, and have further concluded that I am not so poor a horse that they might not make a botch of it in trying to swap." Lincoln's wit has different versions. Including the more popular warning, **don't swap horses in midstream.**

Politically speaking, **to beat a dead horse** means to be persistent about promoting an issue that has no apparent value—a hopeless cause. In the 1800s, Englishman John Bright coined this phrase as flogging a dead horse when he described the efforts of his friend Earl Russell, who petitioned the English Parliament to reduce government spending. Russell's lobbying, according to Bright, was spent in futility, "like flogging a dead horse to rouse Parliament from its apathy."

### Criminal Slang: A Few Chosen Words

**Bagged**: to have done time in prison.

**Barking Iron/ Shooting Iron**: A firearm, most often a pistol.

**Belly through the bush**: when a criminal is on the run from the law.

**Bilk**: to cheat or swindle.

**Blackleg**: a criminal adept at cheating through professional gambling or scamming.

**Boarding School / Calaboose / Cooler**: a prison, jail or other type of long-term confinement.

**Bogus**: a sham or forgery, most often used to describe counterfeit currency or false identity.

**Cold as a wagon tire**: dead.

**Coot**: a lame-minded person, an easy victim for a swindle.

**Grog Shop**: saloon. Also called bucket shop, whisky mill and doggery.

**Hornswoggle**: to cheat as a gambler would at cards.

**Iron Worker**: slang for a thief whose specialty was safe cracking.

**Lynch**: to execute a person by hanging. Also called a necktie social.

**Pinched / Pulled**: caught in a criminal act by the police.

**Ride out on a rail**: when undesirable elements (rowdy persons) are forced to leave town. Usually with the warning to "Get out of town or else…"

**Road Agent**: a highwayman/bandit specializing in robbing stagecoaches and wagons and carriages.

**Rounder**: while a game of rounders is an old-fashioned description for the sport we now call baseball, a person known as a rounder was a habitual criminal—a lifer.

**Scratcher**: a criminal whose specialty is forging documents and currency.

**Sockdologer**: a powerful blow executed by a fist or a weapon such as a club.

**Sugar**: ill-gotten money or jewels.

**Swarthout**: to scam, swindle or cheat a victim and then immediately flee the scene of the crime.

**Touching a jug**: meaning to rob a bank.

**Wake-snake Ruckus**: to make a commotion of activity and noise for the purpose of detracting attention away from a crime in motion.

**Walking Whiskey Vat**: A habitual drunkard considered an easy mark for robbery or scamming.


## Prairie Lawyers Serenade the Night

Following in the wake of the Civil War, the glory years of the American cowboy spanned less than a quarter century; and yet, these western heroes of the open range imprinted their indelible mark in the pages of California history.

In their mannerisms, apparel and—most of all—in their language, cowboys left a rich and colorful legacy. As time passed, many cowboy words and phrases found their way into the twentieth century through the sanctioning of Webster's dictionary. Still, some expressions were kept "under the hat", and circulated only among the trade.

Steeped in the tradition of California's original cowboys: vaqueros throughout the southwest had two major concerns: keeping an eye on the herd and keeping on the good side of the biscuit shooter (cook).

Moving cattle was routine business, but staying in favor with the biscuit shooter required diplomacy. No cowpoke worth his saddle wanted to start the day with graveyard stew (milk toast) when he could sink his teeth into tasty hot rocks (biscuits) and jerky.

A cowboy's life wasn't easy riding. Some kind of commotion was always brewing on the ranch. There was "nothing no-how worse" after a long day of chasing fan tails (wild horses), taming a broom tail (wild mare) and breaking broncos (untamed horses) than to find out too late that there is a nice kitty (skunk) curled up under your bunk; and then trying to sleep when a Rocky Mountain canary (burro) was nitpicking at a prairie lawyer's (coyote) serenade!

On a day off, a cowboy's venture into town fit right in the saddle with its own challenges. If not wise, he might sacrifice his earnings on the high dollar of coffin nails (cigarettes) and coffin varnish (liquor), then end up half shot (drunk) in need of a sawbones's (doctor's) remedy—and with nothing more to show for his hard-earned oats than a prayer book (cigarette papers).

Whatever passed from dawn to dusk, a cowboy couldn't duck out from answering to the laws of the land and laws of the people. Not hankerin' to go over the range (die) before receiving the good words of the local sky pilot (preacher), a cowboy would do his dandiest to avoid hindering the law. From horse thieving to yampin (petty theft), offenders were dealt with swiftly. Why, no cowpoke in his right mind would ride into a dry creek when a dry gulching (public execution by gunfire) was in progress. No, sir, not even an Oklahoma rain (sandstorm) could persuade a rider to take refuge in a creek bed sanctioned as a forum for justice, the risk of accidental lead poisoning (being shot) wasn't worth the shelter.

## Boonville's Conversational Language

California's Route 128 leads from the Mendocino coast into the agriculturally verdant backcountry of Anderson valley. It's a picturesque drive of about forty miles that can be made in a leisurely hour. But don't be fooled by the mileage and driving time factor. In actuality, it's a trek that takes a person back about one hundred years ago to the quaint town of Boonville where residents converse in a language unlike any other in the world.

Boontling, or just "Boont" for short, was the language of preference in Boonville from 1880 to 1920. Nowadays, residents keep the vocabulary alive for the sake of tradition, tourism and little tikes growing up in the one-of-a-kind culture of Boonville.

Supposedly, there isn't a resident in Boonville who can rightly recollect how or why the language was invented in the first place. Some say the Boontling dialect was created so adults could converse about private topics in the presence of children. Yet, others claim the opposite is true; it was Boonville's youth of the 1880s who originated the language in disregard for adult ears. And then there is the story that Boont was born from necessity by women in the village who catered to gossiping tongues.

As a language, Boontling is every bit as mysterious and colorful as any story regarding its origin. Linguists who have studied Boont have categorically surmised the following attributes:

SYNTAX. Boontling's syntax is represented by word formation drawn from the languages of English, Irish, Scottish, with cultural influences from Spanish and regional Pomo Indian.

PHONETICS. Boontners often tweak or reshape phonetic sounds to create unusual, yet mirroring, and germane words. For instance, haircut is hairk.

NAMES and SCRIPTURE are made liberal use of in borrowing from proper names and phrases from the Bible. In Boont, a news reporter is called a Greeley after the famous news journalist Horace Greeley. An orphaned child is named a bulrusher from the Bible story of infant Moses having been stowed away in a basket crafted from bulrushes.

IMITATING REAL SOUNDS is a knack the creators of Boontling excelled at. Using keen ears for real-life sounds, descriptive words mimicked the sounds of everyday things such as when the report of a .22 rifle is called a spat—the sound heard when the rifle is fired.

FIGURE of SPEECH. Boontners have sharp observations regarding the quirkiness of human nature. Hence, a woman with strong preferences for the finer things in life is referred to as a mink.

To hear Boontling spoken by a native Boontner is a rare treat that can only be experienced with a visit to Boonville. Learning how to converse in Boont is a challenge, because the creators never wrote an official dictionary. However, for those interested enough to give speaking Boontling a try, here is an unofficial glossary of some Boont words:

ab chaser – An abalone gatherer/fisherman.

apple-head – girlfriend.

bahler or bahlest – good/better, best.

bahl hornin' – good drinking

belhoon - dollar

bluetail – Rattlesnake

Boont dusties – residents at rest in the Boonville Cemetery.

can-kicky – angry.

Charlie Ball – to deliberately set about to embarrass someone.

chiggrul – food.

deek – to look.

dinklehonk – cow.

gorm – to eat (chiggrul).

harp – to speak Boontling.

hoot – to laugh.

horn – a cup/glass, a drink (beverage) or to drink.

huoottle – hotel.

jeffer – a large fire.

kilockety – to travel on a train.

kiloppety – to travel by horse.

kimmie – a male resident of Boonville.

larrup – to beat the living daylights out of someone or thing.

lews/larmers – gossip.

ling – language.

ose – human buttocks.

ot – to labor hard.

pike – to walk, stroll, mosey or hike.

shoveltooth – doctor.

slug – to sleep.

stook on – in love with.

teem – time.

trashmover – a strong and windy winter storm.

weech – a young child.

zeese – coffee.

# CHAPTER 7
# EARLY CALIFORNIA RECIPES AND FOOD CULTURE

Early Californians grew, hunted, and traded their foods and recipe supplies. In later years, as cities were founded, dry-goods stores, butcher shops and market vendors afforded settlers the convenience of purchasing food and the cooking ingredients required to create a meal. For the most part, these early settlers were luckier than most pioneers—at least once they arrived in California. Due to the majestic diversity in California's terrain, the makings of a good meal were bountiful.

Inland valleys provided an abundance of meat-bearing animals to hunters including grizzly bears, deer and wild fowl that were plentiful. The coastline was a haven for fisherman and even the seemingly barren deserts revealed secrets to survival with hunting of wild hare, birds of prey and rattlesnake. Food, in an array of what now seem unusual sources—from common garden snails that were fed leftover milk to fatten them out of their shells to chicken-fried rattlesnake—was never wasted. Nearly every part of an animal or plant was used to make something edible.

I am often asked how I come by pioneer recipes. The answer is simple and yet complicated. Many recipes listed here, and in my first book, *Southern California Miscellany*, came to me in my general research of California history—a passion of mine for over forty years. And other recipes have been collected, as I made guest-speaker appearances at clubs and organizations, especially those organizations kindred to cuisine or history. Women's clubs and historical societies have always been a trea-sure trove of resources. At these guest-speaker occasions I mention that I collect antique recipes from California's pioneering days and ask any-one with such recipes to share them. The recipes are shared, usually in their original form and often with an historical anecdote that lends fla-vor to the recipe. Many recipes are duplicates. In fact, the vast majority of recipes given to me are duplicates with minor personal changes ren-dering them unique to the person who shared the recipe. For this rea-son, I can rarely give credit to any one person has having the authentic first version of a recipe.

Wherever possible, I present an authentic or original recipe, true to the grammar, spelling and unique phrasing of the pioneer cook who developed the recipe. And, when practical, I list a modern version of the same recipe for contemporary cooks to use. I hope that in listing recipes in this manner it will give all readers the insight into how California pioneers lived. For nothing is so much a telltale sign of how a culture lived as is the cuisine of their time. If for no other reason, I urge all readers of this book to examine these recipes in a thoughtful manner and to try at least one recipe. When you cook with recipes from the past, you present a tasty tidbit of history that can be conveyed in a most digestible way (pun intended)! In other words…Think of these recipes as antiques you can share with family and guests as you serve up a tasty tidbit of food and conversation.

Food history of the 1800s is filled with landmark technologies that we take for granted today. Here's a list of highlights from 1806 to 1906.

1806 - Apple cider recipe and process is patented by Isaac Quintard.

1812 - The first American recipe for tomato ketchup is circulated. However, the general public is skeptical of tomatoes, which are widely believed to be unhealthy. Ketchups are most commonly made from fruits such as prunes or nutmeats such as walnuts. In 1820, scientists proclaim tomatoes are not poisonous and are actually healthy, espe-cially for their high content of Vitamin C. In 1830, tomato ketchup is bottled for commercial markets.

1825 - Preserving food in tins is patented by Ezra Daggett and Thomas Kensett. Their new 'canning' process is spurred by interest in pioneering the American West. Called "airtights" by overlanders heading west in wagon trains, the canned foods most popular with pioneers were corn, potatoes, peas and beans.

1851 - Borden brand evaporated milk is packaged in cans… making milk available to settlers in rural regions.

1866 - Root beer is invented by Charles Elmer Hires.

1869 - Margarine is invented as a butter spread substitute. Other spreads remain popular, including cottonlene, a butter substitute derived as a by-product of cotton production.

1879 - Dry, powdered milk is patented. However, fresh liquid milk is now sold in glass bottles and California's dairy farms expand to meet the need.

1886 - California fruit growers ship their first trainload of fruit—primarily citrus—from Los Angeles to cities in the mid-west. This citrus promotion enhances California's lure and aids in the travel boom to California.

1891 - SPAM, the controversial canned "potted" meat is debuted by the George A. Hormel and Company.

1897 - Housewife May Wait and her carpenter husband Pearle document an original recipe that combines gelatin with fruit juice flavoring. They call their brightly colored new dessert JELL-O.

1899 - The first refrigerating machine designed for home use is patented. Up until this time cooks relied on solid oak iceboxes to keep food from spoiling.

1900 - The quintessential American sandwich: the Hamburger is created.

1906 - The Pure Food and Drug Act, along with the Meat Inspection Act becomes law.

# CHAPTER EIGHT
# BEVERAGES

## Trade Whiskey

Need something to barter with when you're low on cash? The whiskey rendered from this recipe is just that—a commodity worth its weight in gold. Pioneers, cowboys and prairie adventurers alike went through lean times when all they had to bargain with was whatever they had on hand. Alcoholic beverages were often at the top of a wish list, especially at hunting camps and gold fields. Anyone with enough leftover bourbon or whiskey could dilute it to brew up a batch of this lightening juice and end up with gold in his or her pocket.

For today's practicality and safety, this is not a good recipe to try, especially since we now know the dangers of tobacco and gunpowder… unlikely beverage ingredients and a deadly combination in any fashion. Still and all, this recipe is one that speaks volumes about the way people lived. Hence, it's best to savor the flavor of history in Trade Whiskey, and let it be a good topic for conversation.

Original Recipe:

Brew tobacco tea with 1 cup of water, 3 jalapeno peppers, 1 handful of cut tobacco and 1 spoonful sugar—if you have it. Boil hard one minute. Cool and add 2 pinches of black gunpowder. Stir, strain and add any leftover bourbon or whiskeys you have, up to 1 liter, then start recipe over to stretch your whiskey for trading.

**Egg Wine**

This wine served two important purposes. Served warm it took the chill out of a person's bones even on the coldest nights. And, it was a good way to use up the abundance of eggs that just about every pioneer with a coop would have. Think of Egg Wine as a pioneer style of eggnog.

Original Recipe:

After whipping up 4 whole eggs plus an additional 4 yolks, stir in 2 cups sugar. Then add 2 quarts of any good wine, preferably white, put in kettle and heat—while stirring—over medium heat until bubbles rise, but do not boil. Remove, cool, serve while warm.

**Orange Wine**

Considering Californians' passion for citrus fruit, it's not surprising that early citrus pioneers had their own recipes for making wine from the fruit of their orchards and labor. An alternate version of this recipe substitutes honey for the sugar required. I have not attempted a honey-version of this recipe. Not caring much for sweet wines, this recipe is not to my personal taste. However, I've been told that those who prefer a dessert wine enjoyed this recipe and have taken to adding personal touches such as a sprig of mint or a dash of cinnamon.

Original Recipe:

To each 1-gallon of water add 2 and half pounds of sugar. Beat the whites of 2 eggs till frothy and stir them into the water/sugar. Let boil 1 hour. From this take 1 gallon water-sugar mix and add juice and pulp of 8 oranges, pare them very thin. When water is almost cold, marry together both mixtures into large crock and stir in half a palm of active yeast, let stand in cold pantry 2 or 3 days. Stir each day, morning and night. After day 3, strain mixture and bottle with cork. Store cold.

Modern Version:

Ingredients: 1 gallon filtered water. 2 pounds white granulated sugar (no need to measure if you use a 2 pound bag of store-bought sugar). 2

large egg whites, beaten frothy to a soft peak stage. 8 large oranges, juiced with pulp, or approximately 5 cups of prepared orange juice. 1 tablespoon of active dry yeast (used in making breads, can be purchased in flour/sugar section at grocery store).

Directions: In a large saucepan or kettle, pour one gallon of filtered water, add all sugar, and stir to blend. Place pan on stove, over medium heat. Continuously stir mixture until it begins to boil (bubbles break the surface). Add the beaten egg whites and continue stirring mixture on medium heat for 5 minutes then reduce heat to a simmer. Simmer one hour, remove from heat, let cool until slightly warm, add all yeast, stir well, add all orange juice, stir until well blended. Transfer mixture to a glass or plastic container and cover with a breathable material such as a paper towel of tea towel, refrigerate, remembering to stir mixture twice a day for three days. Orange wine may be fermented longer than time specified. Finally, transfer wine to bottle and cap or cork to seal. Keeps in refrigerator up to two weeks. NOTE: the orange juice determines the flavor of this beverage. When serving, Brandy may be added to spike the wine.

**Apple Toddy**

Apples were grown in California before citrus and remain a popular crop, especially in San Bernardino County's premier apple region at Oak Glen, from which this recipe sprouted. Apple Toddy was one of the more complex recipes I had to convert to modern techniques.

Original Recipe:

To 1 gallon of Apple Brandy or Whiskey, add 1 and half gallons of hot water, well sweetened with 2 handfuls sugar, 1 dozen roasted apples, halved and seeded, 2 grated nutmegs, 1 grated allspice ball, 1 grated clove ball, a pinch of mace. Siphon with half pint of good Rum. Let sit 4 days.

Modern Version:

Ingredients: 1 gallon apple brandy/whiskey or for non-alcoholic beverage, use apple cider. 1 and a half gallons of hot filtered water. 1 cup white sugar. 12 apples peeled and cored, cut into quarters. 1 teaspoon each: ground cloves, ground allspice and ground cinnamon.

Directions: In a large stew pot or kettle, using medium heat, warm all the filtered water, until bubbles rise to surface, do not boil. Add sugar, stir until dissolved. Add apple quarters, continue cooking until apples are tender, remove from heat, and add all spices. Cool, refrigerate for 4 days then strain and add half pint of rum. Omit adding rum if you desire this beverage to remain non-alcoholic.

## Citrus and Rum Grog

Disease is responsible for the concoction of this beverage. Simply put, Citrus and Rum Grog was invented to stave off the Seaman's disease known as scurvy. In its early stages scurvy was an aggravating nuisance and, if not treated, the disease withered away at a person's body resulting in swollen gums, pocked flesh, failing bones and jaundice.

British doctors in 1600 made the connection between scurvy and diet. In hopes of preventing the disease, they convinced the British Admiralty that doses of Vitamin C in the natural form of lemon juice would prevent scurvy. The British Navy adopted the recommendation and began dispensing lemon juice mixed with a sailor's daily rum ration to all seamen. According to Navy legend, the first commander to issue this diluted mixture was Admiral Vernon, better known as "Old Grog"—a name earned by his preference for donning a worn grogram cloth cloak during stormy weather.

Old Grog's mixture was hearty enough to make his sailors see fog under sunny skies. Hence, the drunken nature the beverage caused originated the term of one feeling groggy. The anecdote for having sailors too groggy to perform duties was to dilute the mixture. This time, the rum was watered down with water then blended with healthy doses of lemon juice.

The fight against scurvy took a turn for the worse in the mid-1800s when the British began substituting limes for lemons. Containing considerably less Vitamin C than lemon, scurvy began to rear its ugly head once again. The obvious symptoms set British sailors apart from others to the point that Americans began branding them as "limeys."

Original Recipe:

To 1 gallon of rum put in 2 quarts of fresh lemon juice, sweetened with 1 pound refined sugar, to this add the rind of juiced lemons, let stand 7 days, then bottle it off for rationing.

## Tea Punch

Green tea has been taken for centuries as a healthy alternative to caffeine-laden coffee. This recipe was popular with San Francisco's elite society of the 1890s.

Original Recipe:

Brew 3 cups strong green tea to which, add the thinly sliced rind of 6 lemons, one and half pounds sugar, juice of 6 lemons. Stir together a few minutes, then strain. Served over ice.

## Mexican Hot Chocolate

Chocolate, as a beverage and later with European influence as a bar or cake, was introduced to the New World by Spanish explorers of the 1500s who discovered chocolate in Latin America in the form of the indigenous cacao tree. The Latin beverage was made in several steps. First, beans were dried and roasted over fire. They they were pounded into a paste with water and diluted into steaming water. Often regional touches were added such as dried flower petals, as well as hot peppers.

At the end of the sixteenth century in Mexico, small palm-sized cakes of cocoa paste had sugar incorporated into them along with spices such as cinnamon and clove. These little chocolate cakes were the 1500's version of an instant beverage. Add hot water, a little masa (corn flour), beat until frothy, and the cook had a hot invigorating beverage fit for a king—quite literally speaking. For in Mexico, hot chocolate was the preferred beverage of local royalty.

By 1630, nearly every family in Mexico had their own version of a hot chocolate recipe, as exampled in this antique version.

Original Recipe:

Grind 100 roasted cocoa beans; mix in 2 ground pods of chili, a handful of aniseed, the powdered dried petals of 6 roses, and half pound of sugar. Steep all ingredients in boiling water until flavored to liking. Serve warm with fresh cream.

Modern Version:

Ingredients: 9 cups water. One half-cup sugar, 2 tablespoons ground cinnamon, 9 ounces grated Oaxacan chocolate (shop for this kind of chocolate at a Latin/Mexican cultural grocery store) OR use bittersweet baking chocolate. 7 ounces prepared corn tortilla masa (available at cultural grocery store and sometimes in larger supermarkets).

Directions: Using a blender, blend 2 cups of the water with all ingredients until blended. Transfer to large kettle and add the remaining water. Under low heat stir until blended and hot. Remove kettle from heat, let cool, but serve warm. Leftover hot chocolate can be stored in a covered container in refrigerator up to 4 days. Reheat on stove or in microwave.


## Orange Syllabub

Syllabub is a beverage fit for a gala celebration. The name is believed to be a combination of words. *Sillery* from the Champagne region in France, known for its bubbling wines and from "bub," a casual name for a bubbly beverage, dating back to 1537. California's founding Spanish families went to great lengths to lay a lavish table for special events. Measuring up to their high expectation is this lovely to look at and delicious to partake of, Orange Syllabub. This recipe from 1800 is easily prepared for today's celebratory events. This syllabub is best served in a large punch bowl, accommodating at least 12 cups in quantity.

Ingredients:  2 cups of bubbling white wine, 1 cup fine white sugar, Grated rind of 1 orange (4 tablespoons of store-bought grated orange peel), ½ cup orange juice, 3 cups milk, 2 cups cream. For punch bowl topper: Beat 4 large egg whites with ½ cup fine white sugar until stiff and set aside on a cool cupboard (refrigerate until ready to use).

Directions: In a large bowl, combine wine and sugar, stir until all sugar is dissolved. Add to this the orange juice and grated orange rind, stir well. In a separate bowl combine milk and cream, stir well, and then add this mixture to the wine in large bowl. Stir gently to mix well. Transfer syllabub to punch bowl, top with beaten egg whites and sprinkle with nutmeg or cinnamon.

Note: If the punch bowl used is wide at its brim, then you may want to double up on the egg white topper. The presentation will be disappointing if the foam of egg whites does not completely cover the surface of the syllabub. Yet, a different approach is to use a store-bought whipped topping, the type that comes in a tub, then ladle this topping over the syllabub's surface.

## Lemonade

Lemons came to California via a long and winding route of trade and exploration. Native to Asia, this tangiest of all fruit was named by Persians and was first called *limun*. Spanish friars brought lemons with them and once planted, the fruit took root with such phenomenal success that lemon groves sprang up across the state. By the mid-1800s, California was the lemon capital of the nation. Today, California leads the nation in lemon production, followed by Florida and Texas. Lemons are the iconic fruit of childhood. No other fruit has inspired so many kid-sized entrepreneurs… all of whom pitched their own lemonade stand to sell refreshing glasses of lemonade on a hot summer's day.

Original Recipe: For each glass of Lemonade, squeeze ½ a lemon into glass, stir in 1 teaspoon of sugar. Add water and ice. Makes 6 ounces, without ice.

## Sparkling Sangria

Sangria is a Spanish word describing the bleeding red color of this wine. As a drink it was the height of fashion in the 1960s. However, a hundred years prior, sangria was an ordinary beverage, often mixed with the oh-so-trendy sparkling mineral water that was stock in trade for hundreds of health resorts throughout California. This version uses convenient bottled soda water. If you care to lend a flavor of authenticity to this recipe, try grocery hunting for an original California brand of sparkling water such as Calistoga or Arrowhead.

Original recipe: To serve 6 drinks, use a medium punch bowl: Add 1 large orange and 1 large lemon (sliced very thin), 5 strips of cucumber peel, 1 bottle dry red sangria wine, 3 Tablespoons cognac. This may rest in bowl until ready to serve, at which time you should add 8 ounces of iced sparkling mineral water plus enough ice cubes to equal 2 per serving. Stir and serve immediately.

## Ranch Coffee with Egg

Do you long for a rich full-bodied cup of coffee? Put away your drip, percolator or expresso coffee machine and reach for an old-fashioned granite-ware coffeepot that will set uncomplaining on your range top or camp fire. If your coffeepot has a basket, take it out and set it aside. Here's the What and How.

**What:** 1 granite-ware coffeepot, 8 ounces of fresh ground coffee, 1 cup cold water, 1 egg, 6 cups boiling water.

**How:** Make sure coffeepot is clean, any residue from previous servings will spoil the taste. Wash egg, then in a bowl, break and beat egg slightly so yellow and white create a marble. Save eggshell. Next, add ½ cup cold water, crushed eggshell and ground coffee. Put all this in coffeepot, pour in 6 cups boiling water and stir thoroughly. Boil on high heat 3 minutes, remove, stir again and place on back of stove to simmer on lowest heat for 10 minutes, remove and add the remaining ½ cup cold water. Strain into server. Or pour directly from pot with a straining spoon over spout to catch grounds.

## Stovetop Percolator Coffee

This is what coffee used to taste like before electrical coffee makers. It can be percolated on any type of stove. When we lose power to a winter storm, I fire up our wood stove (the same one that heats our house), and in the dead of winter I am not without a warming cup of coffee to hold and sip as I watch snowflakes blanket our mountain forest.

Directions for each cup of coffee: In a granite-ware coffeepot with a percolator basket: Take out metal basket and stem. Fill pot with as many cups of cold water that you want coffee for serving. Measure into the basket the same amount of ground coffee per cup as you would for a drip coffeemaker (rule of thumb is 1 or 2 tablespoons per cup, depending on your preference for strong coffee). Be sure to fit the basket lid tightly, then place pot lid on. Set filled coffeepot on high heat. How soon it will begin to percolate depends on the amount of coffee your making, the size of the pot and intensity of heat. Once the pot begins to percolate, allow one minute of percolation per each cup of coffee. After the allowed time, taste test coffee, if it is as you like, remove basket and stem, keep coffee near heat source to keep warm. If coffee is weak, percolate longer. If coffee is too strong, it is best to add a little water to your drinking cup than to add water to the pot.

## Grape Juice

This beverage is an excellent way to make the most of produce market bargains on California grapes. It can be frozen to enjoy a bit of summer sunshine in winter. Makes a wonderful addition to a holiday dinner.

Original Recipe. 4 quarts of ripe grapes, variety is your choice. 1 quart of cold water. Wash and stem grapes, put in large kettle with water, boil on high heat until soft (mushy). Remove from heat and set aside to cool, cover with a tea towel while cooling. When cool enough to handle, strain grapes and water through a coarse cloth (unbleached muslin from a sewing store is ideal and inexpensive), repeat this process twice. Once juice is extracted, put back in kettle, and warm gently (low heat) for a few minutes, then stir in 1 cup of white sugar for each quart of juice (or add I cup of sugar at a time and taste test to your liking). Stir until all sugar is dissolved then turn heat to high and boil 10 minutes. Remove from heat, cover with pot lid or tea towel. Once cooled, transfer to beverage bottle or pitcher. If you plan to freeze this juice, let it cool overnight in a refrigerator and then transfer it to a freezer-proof container for freezing. Thaw juice overnight in refrigerator.

# CHAPTER NINE
# MEATS

**Calf's Head Stew**

"Waste not…Want not." A tried and true adage practiced every meal-time in early California. Nearly every part of an animal was made edible by pioneers. This recipe exemplifies how a cook made the most of what was offered up for meal making. By today's standards, it could be difficult to get a butcher to sell you a calf's head…but should you come across the opportunity, here's an original recipe to try.

You'll need one calf's head, scrubbed clean from a solution of ¼ lye soap to ¾ parts boiled water. Remove eyes and clean nostrils with a good stiff bottlebrush, then insert head in large bucket, pour in lye/water solution and let sit one hour. What the solution hasn't removed, scrub with a clean cotton cloth or flour sack. Rinse with boiled water. Next, put head in large kettle, cover with cold, clean water and boil gently 5 hours. Skim off scum as it rises. Add 1 large chopped onion, as well as herbs and spices of own liking. Simmer another hour, then add any available vegetables, as you would for any other kind of stew. Stew 'til done. Serve.

**Catfish Chowder**

Unlike a calf's head, today's markets do offer catfish. If your regular grocery market doesn't carry it, check a telephone directory for a fish market. Of course, let's not rule out the possibility you may catch your own. Need an excuse to go fishing?

Original Recipe:

Wash one large catfish in warm water, rinse clean and put in kettle, cover with water. Boil until fish bones flip out. Take out fish and chop it up. Return to kettle with 1 pint of new water. Add large lump of butter, 1 cup of cream, 1 chopped onion, 1 spoon of mustard. Stir and simmer 'til thick, add salt and pepper.

Modern Version:

Ingredients: 4 to 5 pounds of catfish with heads removed. 1 cup butter. 1 cup heavy cream. 1 large onion, chopped. 1 tablespoon of ground mustard (dry mustard powder). Salt and pepper to taste. Water.

Directions: In a large saucepan or deep frying pan, place fish parts in bottom and cover with water. Water should be an inch over the upper-most part of fish. With high heat bring to a quick boil for one minute. Remove fish to a platter, discard water. Using a small sharp knife, care-fully slice fish lengthwise, open and remove all bones. Return fish parts to saucepan and add 2 cups water and chopped onion. Under medium heat, cook 10 minutes until warm, then add heavy cream, butter. Cook another 10 minutes and then add mustard, salt and pepper. Continue on medium heat, stirring to keep mixture blended, until thickened to your liking. To thicken this chowder in a hurry, have one large peeled potato boiled and mashed to very fine texture, and add the mashed potato when adding the mustard, salt and pepper.

## Frog and Snail Soup

Reportedly, this soup made a meal to please the finest guest, but was served up to cure a cold as well. I suppose, if you live in a wetland area frequented by common garden snails and frogs, this recipe is right for your kitchen. Pioneers didn't buy the makings for this soup, they just plucked them from the nearby stream or pond. As for the snails… They were entitled to the best of kitchen leftovers, namely, cream. Shallow plates were filled with cream to feed snails. The snails fattened up on the rich food until they nearly grew out of their shells, plucking the plumped up snails out of their shells was an easy task given to young children. Older children were given the duty of frog catchin' at the local creek.

I'm not about to give you a modern version of this recipe… I've never had the druthers to perfect one. However, the recipe here, in its antique form, speaks quaintly in regard to the creative culinary talents of early Californians.

First, take 20 garden snails, all fattened up from cream and plucked from shells, and grind them in a mortar. Next, take back legs of 30 garden frogs, boil heartily for one minute, cool and skin. Put frog leg meat in with snails and pound together. Put snails and frogs in large pot, cover ¾ with water, boil hard 1 hour. Stir often to prevent sticking. Next, add 12 sliced turnips, 1 bunch of chive or Spanish onions, chopped. Simmer on low heat until turnips are tender. Add a pinch of salt, but not pepper.

**Jack Rabbit Soup**

European settlers who came to California were quite accustomed to eating wild hares. In fact, when rabbit was prepared as a roast, it was considered fit for a king. This version of soup is typical of making do with a European recipe, modified to California style with native Jack Rabbits, which were easily hunted or snared. Words to the wise, if you hunt for rabbits, follow this old adage: Eat varmints only after the first hard frost of winter. The weak ones die out in severe frost because their bodies are racked with parasites. Come spring, let the first generation go unharmed to render offspring.

Original Recipe:

Butcher heads of 2 rabbits and skin body parts. Wash, dust with flour and fry 'til brown in skillet of hot fat. Remove and put into stew pan. Cover Rabbit parts with water, boil gently 1 hour. Add vegetables of own liking with a pinch of dry mustard, then add sliced rind of 1 lemon and pepper to your taste. Stew 3 hours or 'til vegetables are tender.

Modern Version:

Some country-styled butcher shops sell farm-fed rabbit meat. Or check a telephone directory for a rabbit farmer. In the early 1900s, the area in Riverside County known as Sunnymeade (now called Moreno Valley,) was a popular area for rabbit farming.

Ingredients: 4 pounds skinned rabbit meat parts. 1 cup of flour for dusting. 1 teaspoon dry mustard powder. 1 lemon, (thoroughly clean the exterior in warm water, peel and dice rind.) 1 pound carrots shredded. 3 large celery stalks sliced 1 inch thick. 6 large new potatoes (peeled or not), diced to bite size. 1 cup of olive oil for frying. Salt and pepper to taste.

Directions: Rinse rabbit parts in cool water, pat dry with paper towel. Place flour in bowl and place meat, one part at a time in flour, turn to coat each side. Pour olive oil into a large skillet, and begin to heat on medium temperature, about 2 minutes. Transfer flour-dusted rabbit parts to skillet to brown on all sides. When browned, remove meat and place on paper towels to drain excess oil. Transfer to large saucepan, cover meat with water and stew on low-medium heat for 3 hours, stirring oc-casionally. When meat is tender, add prepared vegetables, mustard, and lemon peel. Continue cooking until potatoes are done, add salt and pep-per to taste. If you are adventurous enough to try this dish… know that this recipe is mild in flavor and can be adapted to personal preferences. For instance, adding garlic and onions will strengthen the flavor or add diced hot peppers to spice it up!


**Coffee Pot Roast**

This recipe was an excellent way for a ranch cook to use up leftover coffee that's been sitting over the fire a bit too long. Brew up some extra strong coffee for this recipe.

Original Version:

Take 4 pounds of beef rump roast to sear in hot fat. Put in Dutch oven with 1/3 pot of strong coffee, 2 cups water, 2 pours of red wine, 1 large onion, chopped and 2 cloves garlic, mashed. Cook on medium fire an half an hour, stir often. Then reduce heat and cover to simmer 'til meat is tender, about 2 hours or more. If you like it thickened and sweet, add some tomato paste or ketchup.

Modern Version:

Ingredients. One 4-pound beef rump roast. 2 cups extra strong coffee. 2 cups water and ½ cup red wine or cooking sherry. 1 large onion, sliced thin. I small can tomato paste. 1 teaspoon garlic powder. Oil for searing.

Directions. In large roasting pan or Dutch oven, on top of stove, sear all sides of roast in hot oil until browned. Remove from heat. Take roast from pan, drain oil out of pan and return roast to pan. In a large bowl combine water, coffee, red wine, tomato paste and garlic powder, stir to blend then pour over roast. Add sliced onion. Cover pan with lid or foil and bake in preheated 375-degree oven on middle rack 3 to 4 hours, roughly 1 hour per every pound of roast. Stir occasionally while baking.


**Pork and Egg Pudding**

This recipe was a common dish that afforded a handy way to use surplus eggs and leftover pork. Nearly every cook had his or her own style of making Pork and Egg Pudding. It's an antique version of a crustless quiche, pioneer style.

Put slices of ham or pork in a deep baking dish that has been buttered, laying them in rows, crosswise. Make a pudding batter with six eggs, beaten lightly and from a separate bowl, beat together a pint of cream and a pint of flour. Next add eggs to this mixture. Beat well and pour over meat in baking pan. Bake quickly.

Modern Version:

This contemporary version uses cottage cheese instead of cream, and breadcrumbs instead of flour.

Ingredients: Leftover slices of cooked pork, ham or bacon, enough to cover the bottom of a buttered 13x9x2 inch baking pan. 8 eggs, beaten with whisk or spoon, until well blended, 2 cups of cottage cheese: whole, low fat or non-fat. 2 cups of medium fine breadcrumbs, any kind will do. (The type of bread used may enhance flavor.)

In a large bowl, use a whisk or spoon to beat 8 eggs until creamy, add all cottage cheese, mix well with spoon, add breadcrumbs, and mix well. Distribute this mixture over the meat, which has been arranged to cover the bottom of baking pan. Bake at 350 degrees on middle rack in a preheated oven. Baking time varies (35 to 50 minutes) depending on metal or glass pan and gas or electric oven. Check in 20 minutes and every 10 minutes thereafter until casserole is lightly browned and set. Slice into portions and lift out of pan with spatula. Garnish with shredded cheese, salsa or sour cream.

### Barbecued Squirrel

This antique recipe presumes the cook has already beheaded and skinned the squirrels used for this delicacy. I do not have a modern equivalent for this dish. Simply stated, on average, the only squirrels I come across are the unfortunate victims of my driving.

However, there is one very-much-alive squirrel in my life. Her name is Lily. She is a large mountain gray squirrel and has been a welcomed visitor to our Forest Falls home for four years. Lily came to us her first summer. She was ragged and skinny. She seemed wary of us, but our peanuts won her over. That fall, she tangled with some other critter and showed up one morning looking the worse for the encounter. Sporting a nasty wound on her muzzle that showed raw tissue all the way to the bone, Lily looked as if her life was over. My husband Christopher and I took an intense interest in her welfare and fed her a diet of high quality nutmeats… the ones we purchased for our own consumption. By first snowfall she was on the mend and made regular visits in between storms. Lily is still with us, content to be the outdoorsy member of our family. Her persistence to stay with us is evident in the way she always returns when we arrive home from vacation. Lily does not take offense to the fact that we need to get away once in a while.

Original Recipe:

Lay slabs of heavily laden bacon (bacon that is heavy with fat) in pan and put squirrel meat on top. Lay 2 slabs of bacon over meat. Cook in oven until tender to the fork. In next pan, pour in the bacon fat from first pan. Sprinkle 1 palm of flour (approximately ¾ cup) in and brown it. Pour in 1 teacup of water (6 0z) with 2 pats butter and Walnut catsup for flavor. Pour over squirrels and serve.

Note: Pioneers used many types of catsup (ketchup) other than the tomato variety that is common today.

## Chinese Shrimp and Rice

The initial wave of Chinese immigration began in small numbers in 1847. Due to the reliable and hardworking labor ethics of the Chinese, they were employed in various jobs requiring backbreaking work and tedious long hours. It is by no coincidence that Chinese workers made up the majority of laborers who built the Central Pacific Railroad. Under the auspice of railroad magnate Charles Crocker, fifteen thousand Chinese laborers were imported in 1867 to work on building the railroad. Chinese laborers proved to be the unsung heroes of the railroad industry that opened California up to expedited rail travel. The Chinese population grew significantly in the following years, but not without great strife.

By 1867, an additional twenty-two thousand Chinese immigrants arrived at California ports, and the Chinese population continued to increase annually. More often than not, Chinese immigrants succeeded in building a new life in California in contrast to the horrible conditions forced upon them. Racial discrimination against them ran rampant in the 1800s and into the 1900s. Anti-Chinese campaigns such as the "Yellow Peril" and "California for Americans" were constant reminders to Chinese that while they were valued as railroad laborers, they were not welcomed to much else. In the 1850s, they suffered terrible discrimination as witnessed in San Francisco's 1855 Pigtail Ordinance, which decreed that any Chinese man convicted of a crime—regardless of seriousness—would be subjected to having his pigtails sheared off. The cutting of a man's hair, for the Chinese, was demeaning beyond any statute of their cultural law. However, the worst transgression against fairness to Chinese citizens happened in Los Angeles in 1871, when race riots resulted in an all out massacre of twenty Chinese, and the injustice was ignored by the law.

All things considered, Chinese immigrants have given immeasurable sacrifices to the benefit of California. Their culture is one of honorable work ethics balanced with an abiding love of family. Chinese cuisine was easily adapted to California's offerings and tastes. This authentic recipe for shrimp and rice, presented here unchanged, is as easily prepared today as it was over a hundred and fifty years ago.

Original recipe:

1-pound of shrimp, shelled and deveined (ask your meat grocer or purchase frozen shrimp, then thaw and drain). 2 teaspoons of corn starch. Oil for frying (1/2 cup).

6 cups cooked long grain white rice. 4 Tablespoons of soy sauce. Chop fine: 1 hot pepper, 2 Spanish onions, including ½ green stalk of each onion. 6 beaten and scrambled eggs.

Dice shrimp, mix with corn starch, and then fry (on medium heat) in hot oil until shrimp turn pink. Remove shrimp from pan (drain on paper towel), leave oil in pan. Into same pan, fry onions and pepper until tender (on medium heat, about 5 minutes). Next, turn down heat, add cooked rice and soy sauce, stir and then add shrimp and eggs. Stir 1 minute—Serve.


**Menudo**

This is the most basic of Mexican soups, claimed to have as many variations as there are cooks in Mexico. Menudo is not only a delicious, hearty meal, but for generations its claim to fame has been its curative properties. Much as with the old adage that the hair of a dog will cure a hangover, Menudo is said to cure not only a hangover, but the common cold as well. No wonder it is a holiday favorite… for the day of feasting and the day after for recovery!

Menudo uses beef tripe… a hold over from Mexico's ancient past when every bit of an animal was used for nutritional value as well as practical purposes. The Spanish Conquistators introduced beef cattle to native Mexicans. As with other original recipes not requiring a great amount of modernization, I have listed modern adaptations in parenthesis within the context of the original recipe. This soup freezes well, so cook up a large batch of it to enjoy now and freeze to serve later on a chilly day.

Original recipe:

Rinse 5 pounds of beef tripe in cold water, drain and cut into bite-sized pieces. Put tripe in large kettle, cover well with water and add 1 Tablespoon salt, 2 chopped onions, 5 cloves garlic (mashed), pinch cumin (1 teaspoon ground cumin), palm chili powder (½ cup ground chili powder), and 1 small hot pepper, finely chopped. Cover and cook (low-medium heat) about 3 hours (meat should be tender). Add 1 large can of drained hominy (or about 2 cups of cooked drained hominy). Simmer (30 minutes). Serve.

Menudo lends itself nicely to incredible personalization. Variations in the kind and amount of peppers, the addition of cooked pinto beans or even fresh cilantro are good starting points for experimentation. You can easily turn this recipe into a signature meal of your own.

## Sagamite

From the Virginia colony of the 1600s to exploration of the Great Lakes, down the Mighty Mississippi to New Orleans and onward to the Westward Expansion… Sagamite is a meat-and-porridge dish that each culture has inherently made its own. Reported to be an Indian name, the word itself as been corrupted so often that its authentic origin is beyond discovery. Sagamite recipes are prominent in Confederate cookbooks and a heavily sweetened hard tack version was used throughout the War Between the States. Unlike Southerners who used hominy grits with brown sugar, more common to California is this Mexican version using corn meal. A modern version follows.

Original Recipe:

Cornmeal, boiled until cooked. Meat added along with fat for seasoning. Add cooked and mashed squash or sweet potatoes—said to satisfy hunger and invigorate the body!

Modern Version:

In a large saucepan: Cook 3 parts cornmeal to 1 part water on low heat until thick. You may also follow directions on corn meal package to make a thick porridge or meal. For an authentic flavor, use Mexican styled corn meal known as "masa" as is used in making tamales. Next, to the thickened corn meal add 2 cups of cooked savory meat such as bacon or ham. If the meat is fried in its own fat, use the fat as well. Stir well. If dry, and you have not used meat fat—add a little olive oil or butter. Next you must decide if you want a sweet Sagamite or a savory dish. For a sweet version add 1 cup of cooked mashed sweet potatoes (1 small can of yams, mashed with the liquid from the can). To sweeten further, add brown sugar. Savory version… Finely chop 2 onions and fry in small amount of oil or fat, drain, add to Sagamite with 1-teaspoon ground black pepper, and salt to taste. Remember, Sagamite is a basic meal, not a gourmet dish!

## Citrus Roasted Pork

Pork was among one of the most useful meats to California's early pioneers. Recipes and *cook's books* of the period wasted no words in issuing accolades to the cook who prepared pork. A generalized survey from cook's writings in 1890 had this to say about pork:

From tip of snout to tip of tail, a fine porker is the premier meat for utilizing every morsel.

Pork's value is that it cooks itself. (Reference to cooking pork in its own juices).

With fine salt pork in the larder, a cook is never without the makings of a satisfying meal.

Pioneers took to heart this well-circulated advice and wasted no time custom fitting pork recipes unique to California's agricultural offerings. No finer recipe, than the one presented here, does justice to pioneer creativity of combining pork with California citrus.

Ingredients:

2 large loins of pork (equal to 6-8 large chops per loin).

6 Tablespoons each of honey and butter (combine by stirring honey into soft butter to form a paste).

1 Teaspoon of ground ginger (stir into honey-butter paste).

3 large sweet onions chopped into eighths.

1 large (or 2 small) Lemons (do not peel) slice thin.

1 large Orange, prepared same as Lemon.

1 Cup Orange Juice combined with ½ Cup Lemon juice and ½ Cup water.

2 Cups of meat or vegetable broth.

Directions: Preheat oven to 400 degrees. Use a roasting pan that will accommodate both loins placed as an arch lengthwise, each loin facing the other to form arch in roasting pan.

Next: Use brush or spatula to spread honey-butter paste over entire roast. Spread chopped onions around sides of loins, encircling roast on all sides. Place slices of oranges and lemons over roast in alternating pattern. Place in oven, uncovered, and roast for 30 minutes at 400 degrees. Remove from oven and pour the Orange/Lemon juice and water mixture into pan, disturbing it evenly around pork. Lightly baste with this liquid. Reduce oven to 350 degrees and continue roasting for an additional 2 hours, baste roast with the pan juices every 30 minutes.

When roast is done, remove to presentation platter. Skim juices from pan and serve separately in sauceboat.

## Veal Kidney with Pine Nuts

The regional addition of using pine nuts in this veal dish is an enhancement made possible by the native people of California. Many of California's native tribes knew how to use indigenous plants to their best advantage and they shared their knowledge with pioneers. Using pine nuts in this recipe is a perfect example of the culinary expertise of:

Luiseno from Southern California's coast.

Cahuilla from the greater basin below the San Bernardino Mountains.

Gabrielino from the greater Los Angeles basin.

Chumash from Santa Barbara's region.

And the Miwok who lived in the region of San Francisco and Monterey.

The original recipe: Prepare sauce first by melting 2 tablespoons of butter in a saucepan over low heat, add next 1 finely chopped medium onion, sauté onion in butter until onion is soft and begins to appear clear. Next, stir in 2 cups of beef broth, ¼ teaspoon of sugar and 1 tablespoon of prepared yellow mustard. Once the mustard is stirred in, remove from heat and set aside.

Now prepare veal: In a large frying pan melt 3 tablespoons butter and sauté 1 small finely chopped onion for one minute, until softened. To this, add 4 thinly sliced veal kidneys and sauté quickly (raise heat to medium high) until redness disappears. Reduce heat to previous setting and stir in ½ cup of dry red wine then stir in the previously prepared broth sauce with ½ cup of pine nuts. Stir for one minute on low heat. Remove and serve kidneys in sauce over rice or mashed potatoes.


## Chicken Cilantro Croquettes

On the subject of chicken ranches... Many Californians of the early 1900s prospered from the population boom by buying a few acres of sunny land and putting up chicken coops. Consequently, chickens were the birds of blue-plate specials throughout the state. Two examples, regionally far apart, and yet in practice much the same, were the communities of Petaluma to the north and Fontana, in the south.

Petaluma's chicken ranch legacy began in the early 1900s when a small group of of Jewish farmers found the region agreeable to raising chickens. In time, farming and Jewish culture combined to create a region unmatched in egg and poultry production and a cultural community with close-knit ties.

About the same time, further south in Fontana, chicken ranches were so successful, that the city paid tribute to its *eggstravagant* history by including the depiction of chicken ranches on the official city seal.

This original recipe dates to Los Angeles of 1905 and is from the family of Miss C. Hernstein.

Directions: To 1 quart of chopped cold chicken, add 2 Tablespoons of chopped dried cilantro. 2 teaspoons salt. ¼ teaspoon of grated nutmeg. 1 Tablespoon of dried onion flakes. 1 Saltspoon (1/8 teaspoon) of ground red pepper. Mix all of the above thoroughly and set aside. Next, into a large sauce pot pour one pint of milk and add to it a paste formed from rubbing together 2 Tablespoons of soft butter with 1 tablespoon of flour. Put this milk mixture on medium heat and stir constantly until it thickens, remove from heat, let cool a few minutes then pour thickened milk over the chopped chicken mix, which you have set aside. Mix well, then let cool until it can be handled and formed into croquettes. To make croquettes, flour your hands and gently pull out a palm size ball of chicken mixture. Flatten slightly, dip into a beaten egg, and roll in breadcrumbs. Make all the chicken mixture into croquettes then get a large frying pan hot with oil. Oil needs to be at least 1 inch deep. Gently place as many croquettes in the pan as possible, yet leaving a little space between each. Fry in hot oil for a minute or two until browned, then use a spatula to carefully turn each croquette over. Once browned on both sides, lift croquettes out of oil, one by one, drain on tea towel (paper towels). Use all the chicken mix up, or store in icebox for up to 3 days to use for another meal. These croquettes are usually served with creamed green peas (cooked peas in sour cream).

## Mole De Guajolote (Turkey in Mole Sauce)

Few recipes can measure up to this one for the dining pleasure of providing an entrée that is as rich in flavor as it is history. Hearkening back to the Mexican roots of colonial California, Mole De Guajolote resonates with the rich cultural legacy of the mighty Aztec nation.

Ever since an Aztec chief first welcomed a Spanish conquistador with an exquisite meal of succulent turkey, the turkey has characterized the depth and sincerity of Mexican hospitality. Of course, the Aztec's honorable efforts had little (if any) positive effect on the intentions of the invading Spanish explorers.

Nonetheless, the turkey remains an icon of hospitality in Mexican households throughout Mexico and California, and as an entrée this recipe is often the meal of choice on holiday gatherings. Many Mexican families still hold true to original customs involving the value placed on turkeys in their culture. Example of such practices include the Zapotecs, who validate a marriage ceremony only after the groom offers up three turkeys accompanied by all ingredients necessary to make mole sauce. And in Veracruz, the dearly departed are celebrated with a feast of turkey and mole; thus guaranteeing the departing soul is well provided for on their heaven-sent journey.

However, you need not wait for a wedding or a wake to enjoy this dish. Turkey is the trendy diet meat of our health-conscience era, and there is no harm in spicing it up a bit with a few hot peppers and combining that fire with the decadence of dark chocolate.

Still not convinced you should try this dish? Think of doing so in answer to the refrain… "Turkey, again"? How often have you tried to do something different with turkey? Now you can.

Ingredients:

10 pounds of turkey parts (choose a mix or all of one kind of your favorite part).

1 cup bacon fat (Vegetable shortening or Olive oil may be substituted).

2 onions chopped.

1 teaspoon of minced garlic.

6 tomatoes, peeled, seeded and chopped (or canned whole stewed tomatoes, drained and equal to 3 cups once chopped).

2 serrano green peppers (or any other hot pepper), do not peel, chop fine.

2 teaspoons of ground cumin powder.

1 teaspoon salt.

½ teaspoon powdered aniseeds (or powdered sassafras root or licorice root).

4 Tablespoons of toasted sesame seeds.

1 cup unsalted roasted peanuts.

¼ cup chili powder.

¼ teaspoon ground cinnamon.

Pinch of ground black pepper (about ¼ teaspoon).

4 corn tortillas cut into small pieces.

3 ounces bitter chocolate (do not use sweetened chocolate or a candy bar). Use a solid-style baking chocolate found in grocery stores on the flour/sugar aisle, or worth a trip to a cultural specialty store to get imported Mexican chocolate).

3 cups turkey broth.

Directions: You will need at least one very large covered skillet and a blender.

1. Put turkey parts in a large skillet and cover with salted water (2 tablespoons of salt to one skillet). Cover and cook on top of stove under medium heat until turkey is done. Cooking time varies depending on size and quantity of parts. On the average, it will take 70 to 90 minutes. When done, transfer turkeys parts to paper towels and pat dry. Discard the salted cooking water. Next, in large skillet, melt ½ the amount of bacon fat and brown turkey parts on all sides. Once browned, put turkey parts aside in shallow pan/plate to keep warm, or at least at room temperature. Save the fat left in skillet.

2. In same skillet used for browning turkey, brown the chopped onions and sprinkle with the minced garlic. Remove from heat and let stand a few minutes to cool, leave in fat.

3. To make Mole paste in a large blender, place in blender the warm

onion-garlic-fat mixture and add all other ingredients EXCEPT turkey broth. Blend at medium-high speed until the mixture is turned into a paste (mole). Depending on the blender size, you may need to blend the mole a little at a time. If so, after each blending, transfer the mixture to a large bowl, so all of it can be stir-blended (using a large spoon) as a final step to guarantee mole paste is thoroughly blended.

4. In large skillet, add remaining ½ cup of fat and warm slightly under medium heat, then add all of the mole paste. Stir constantly to heat mole paste, reduce heat and then slowly stir in the 3 cups of turkey broth. Once broth and mole paste are thoroughly blended, carefully place turkey parts into skillet and spoon mole sauce of parts. Cover skillet and simmer about 30 minutes. Stir occasionally to prevent scorching. Serve over rice. Serves 8 to 10.

### Russian Hunter's Meat Dinner

This recipe could also be called: How to Have a Romance Over Dinner. Okay, so this is a bit of a tease, but the legacy of this dish does have a romantic story that began once upon a time (1806, to be exact) in a land far away.

Russian Count Nikolai Petrovich Rezanov was sent to Spain's province in northern California to buy supplies and to quietly scout out the region in regards to its potential for the fur trade. Furs were Rezanov's utmost concern, for aside of being a count; he dabbled with the title of business executive for the Russian-American Company.

Rezanov's mission was problematic from the get-go. According to California law under the title of Spain, trading with Russia was illegal. As if that were not enough, Spain was keeping a keen eye on the Russians. The Spanish throne was well aware that its chokehold on the Promised Land called California was weakening and by no means did Spain want to give an inch to any other country that was looking to get a foothold on their prized territory. Not to be discouraged, Rezanov's strong will was tempered by a goodly amount of charm that allowed him an audience with the commandant of San Francisco's Presidio. During the course of daily visits, the Russian count did his best to plead his case for purchasing supplies. His charm was deflected and his words went unheard until one day... When he fell in love.

Professing his adoration for the commandant's daughter garnered the count full attention from the Presidio's officials. All of fifteen years old and swept off her feet in love with Rezanov, Dona Concepcion Arguello persuasively argued in favor of marrying her fifty-something-year-old count. In the name of romance (and commerce) the laws were bent, the marriage agreed to, and Rezanov left with the supplies he dearly needed. One hitch stood in the way of the lover's happiness. Dona Concepcion, a Roman Catholic must first receive the blessings from The Vatican in Rome. And Count Rezanov needed permission from his Tsar as well as the Eastern Orthodox Church in Russia. And in the meantime, Rezanov was ordered to set sail for Russia with the purchased supplies.

Count Rezanov never went back to marry his starry-eyed girl. He died enroute to Russia. According to popular legend, Dona Conception did not learn of his death for several years. The manner in which she lived the rest of her life is controversial. Skeptics say she parlayed her "widowhood" into a happy life of social gatherings and social work sponsoring many charity events. Others, who lean toward a romantic ending, prefer to believe she spent her life in grief as a recluse with a broken heart.

One thing is for sure, while in California, Count Rezanov enjoyed the numerous activities and entertainments the region afforded him. Not the least of which was hunting.

He harbored an insatiable curiosity for the region's natural bounty of wild game and fascinating agriculture. This recipe uses both. The wild game called for is adaptable to venison or bear (or if you prefer, beef roast or flank steak), however, the wild juniper berries are a must-have ingredient and may be purchased at specialty stores or herb shops.

Directions: Slice 2 pounds of wild game meat into ¼ inch slabs. In a large skillet, fry meat in ½ cup of bacon fat (or shortening) so it is browned on both sides. To this add 3 chopped onions and 1 pound of sliced mushrooms and 1 cup of broth (meat or vegetable), reduce heat, cover and stew for 10 minutes. Next add 3 large carrots, sliced 1 inch thick and 1 and ½ pounds of scrubbed potatoes (in their skins), sliced thick and ½ cup of juniper berries (Juniperus californica). Cover and simmer until vegetables are tender.

**Lamb Chops with Epigrams**

Cooking lamb chops with literary style and culinary flare is the very essence of this dish. It was common practice in the 1700s and 1800s to provide scintillating topics of conversation when serving a dinner. It is believed, in the archives of culinary lore, that this dish originated in France when an educationally challenged marquise learned that guests at a neighboring estate had dined on a feast of excellent epigrams. Not to be bested, the marquise demanded his cook should create as spectacular a meal for his weekend guests. When the knowledgeable chef attempted to explain that to dine on epigrams meant for the host to present and carry a lively topic of conversation utilizing the literary tool of epigrams, the marquise would have nothing to do with the cook's silliness. In the end, and to save his own livelihood, the wise cook came up with a menu item that pleased his less-than-lettered marquise: Epigramme D'Agneau.

California's premier *epigramest* was none other than Ambrose Bierce. Better known as Bitter Bierce, the acid-tongue journalist and author, he kept his readers turning pages as quickly as he could pen sarcastic opinions. No topic was sacred to Bierce and epigrams were a favorite tool. One work that is exemplary of his best example of epigrams is *The Devil's Dictionary*. Bierce's dictionary is filled with sarcasm, satire and in few cases, truths too raw for any other writer to dare set in ink.

Bierce loved Europe and spent months there writing back to his American cousins about the superiority of European society and especially cuisine. He finally returned home to San Francisco, but the years wore thin on him and in 1913, he left for Mexico to offer his journalistic expertise to Pancho Villa. After crossing over into Mexico, Bierce was never seen or heard from again.

Ingredients: 8 lamb rib chops, 4 Tablespoons of melted butter, 1 large onion (chopped), Bouquet garni (1 garlic clove, 1 bay leaf, 4 sprigs parsley, 3 sprigs cilantro, 6 crushed peppercorns, ¼ teaspoon thyme, tied in a cheesecloth), 1 and ½ cups beef broth, 3 large eggs (well beaten), 1 cup fine dry bread crumbs, ½ cup sweet butter (unsalted butter).

Directions: In a large skillet, place the 4 Tablespoons of melted butter on medium heat and brown all lamb chops on both sides very briefly, reduce heat to a simmer and add chopped onion, Bouquet garni, beef broth. Cover and simmer for one hour or until lamb is tender. Remove skillet from heat. Remove chops to a platter to cool. Strain broth liquid into a saucepan, put aside. (All of the aforementioned may be done a day before and place chops and broth in refrigerator for storage overnight). Have the beaten eggs in a shallow bowl, dip cooled chops one at a time into eggs, then dredge in breadcrumbs, place chops on a platter until all are ready. In a large skillet, melt the sweet butter under medium high heat, if the butter begins to smoke, reduce heat. Place chops in skillet and fry until browned on each side. In meantime, place saucepan of beef broth on a back burner and heat slowly. When chops are fried, transfer them to serving platter with the broth in a gravy boat on side.

# CHAPTER TEN
# VEGETABLES and TOMATOES

## Spanish Rice

This is the most basic of Spanish recipes. Master it, and then personalize the recipe to make it your own specialty. Spanish rice was to early Californians a staple side dish. It is a versatile accompaniment to any meal—morning, noon or night.

Original Recipe:

Take enough rice for each serving and fry it in fat until browned. Add water, boil until soft. Drain, then add onions to the fat, brown them, and mix this with 3 or 4 cut-up tomatoes and some chopped peppers. Add all this to the cooked rice, bake in buttered dish until done.

Modern Version:

Ingredients: 2 cups cooked long grain rice—follow rice package directions. Set aside rice. 1 onion, chopped fine. 1 bell pepper, or any other pepper of your choice, chopped fine. 2 cups of canned crushed tomatoes. ½ teaspoon each of salt and pepper. ¼ teaspoon garlic powder. Butter, oil or fat for browning.

Directions. Before cooking rice according to brand directions—sear the uncooked rice in a pan of hot oil until browned. Drain on paper towels. Then cook according to brand directions. Next, brown chopped onions and pepper in hot oil, transfer to large bowl and combine with cooked rice and all other ingredients. Stir to blend, transfer to a buttered casserole dish with a lid. Cover and bake on middle rack in a preheated

350-degree oven for 20 to 30 minutes. Do not over bake or rice will be dry or it will breakdown and turn mushy.

## Chupe, Mexican Styled

Chupe is a traditional Peruvian corn and potato chowder soup that usually calls for the addition of shrimp or chicken. This Mexican version is vegetarian and is a satisfying bowl of soup all on its own, or for meat eaters, serve this as an accompaniment.

Original Recipe:

In large skillet, lightly brown 1 chopped onion in small amount of fat (olive oil). Take off heat and add a large pinch (1 teaspoon ground) of Mexican paprika and a small pinch (½ teaspoon ground) of cayenne. Stir until onions are stained (take on the color of the paprika and cayenne). In large soup pot, put onions with 2 cloves garlic (mashed or minced), 2 cups vegetable broth (canned or from a reconstituted powder), 3 large potatoes, scrubbed and cut large (do not skin, dice into bite-sized pieces), 2 large ears of sweet corn, sliced thick (after cleaning the ears, leave intact and slice each ear into 1 inch thick slices or "wheels" of corn), a handful of chopped fresh cilantro (usually this is equal to one "bunch" as sold fresh in grocery stores. Use only the flowered ends and a little bit of stalk). Bring all this to a boil over stove (medium heat), potatoes should be tender. Take off fire and pour in large quantity of milk (1 and ½ to 2 cups fresh milk). Simmer until done (corn will be tender). Salt to taste. Consider adding cooked or canned beans.

## Stewed Corn and Beets

An unusual and colorful combination—this recipe pays heed to beets, which have been used for tinting fabrics and as a source of sugar since the 1800s when Californians found that importing sugar cane from Hawaii was cost prohibitive.

California led the nation in beet sugar manufacturing beginning with the nation's first successful factory founded by brothers Ebenezer and Ephraim Dyer in 1869. Situated on the banks of Alvarado Creek in Alameda County, the factory began processing regionally grown beets into sugar on November 15, 1870. Because the railroad had yet to be built in Alvarado, supplies were shipped to the factory—and sugar shipped from the factory—by boat along the creek. Most of the processed sugar was sent to San Francisco.

Following the success of sugar beet farming and processing, farms and factories soon sprang up throughout the state, including regions near the ports of San Francisco, Los Angeles, Long Beach and San Diego.

After Hawaii was admitted to the Union, sugar cane became more affordable and the processing of beet sugar gradually declined. The Dyers' original operation underwent many transitions, the last of which was known as Holly Sugar Company. One of the most successful beet sugar operations closed its doors in 1975.

Original Recipe:

Take 4 ears of sweet yellow corn and cut corn from cob. Put in large pot with lid and to this add 4 peeled and diced beets, 4 Tablespoons butter, 4 cups water. Let cook about 35 minutes (Medium heat, until corn and beets are tender). Season to taste with honey or salt, if you like savory flavors instead.

**Peppers, Tomatoes and Squash**

Take a buttered baking dish (medium size casserole pan) and layer the following: First (bottom layer) 8 green peppers sliced in quarters lengthwise, 6 small Italian squash, sliced into thick circles (1/2 inch thick) and 6 tomatoes, sliced as thick as squash. Over this pour pan drippings (bacon fat or melted butter, about 3 tablespoons) and some salt (lightly sprinkle over top). Bake in moderate oven (350 degrees, preheat) for lesser part of an hour (30 minutes). NOTE. Grated Parmesan cheese is a wonderful topper for this. Sprinkle it on when casserole is first taken out of the oven.

## Spinach with Rhubarb

Spinach, already cleaned and bagged from your grocery market makes this recipe convenient. If you buy spinach in bulk, be sure to clean it well. Putting the loose leaves in a large watertight plastic bag filled with water and then lightly rotating the bag in your hands is an easy way to clean spinach. Drain the leaves well before using in this recipe.

Original Recipe:

Boil 2 pounds of washed spinach leaves in water until tender (10 to 15 minutes), then drain off water. Again in water, boil 3 cups of cleaned and cut rhubarb for 5 minutes, then drain off water. In saucepot, put a few pats of butter (1/4 cup or use same amount of olive oil) to melt slowly (low heat), then add spinach and rhubarb together. Stir and cook to coat with butter for 5 minutes and add seasoning of your own choice.

## Dandelions and Eggs

And to think… most Californians look at dandelions as nothing more than a weed harboring a grudge over their neatly trimmed grassy lawns. Not so with pioneering Californians who knew the edible value of this common "weed."

Other than in your own back yard, dandelions can be found in health food stores and specialty markets. Be cautious before picking them from the ground if you do not know if they are free of pesticides or any other garden and lawn chemicals.

Original Recipe:

Boil a bunch of dandelions (4 pounds washed in cold water) in salted water for 20 minutes (medium-high heat). Drain water. Meanwhile have hardboiled eggs (4 large eggs) skinned and cut (quartered or sliced, keep them apart as individual servings). Put dandelions is soup pan with 1 cup buttermilk, salt and pepper (to taste) and bit of ginger (1 teaspoon ground ginger), cook hard 3 minutes. Take off stove. Into bowls divide the dandelion mixture, and top off each bowl with a 1-egg serving of the quartered/sliced hardboiled eggs. Note, instead of ginger, consider using curry powder. (Serves 4.)

## Potato and Wine Salad

Not enough mayonnaise in your cupboard, or perhaps, as with early Californians, you just don't want to bother to make up a fresh batch of mayonnaise? Here's a potato salad recipe that utilized an ingredient nearly all pioneer households in early California had on hand... locally processed wine. For a non-alcoholic version, try using wine vinegar or one of the new types of non-alcoholic wines available at specialty markets.

Original Recipe:

Take 1 potato per serving desired and scrub clean but leave skin on (6 potatoes equal 6 servings). Cut potatoes into bite sized chunks and put them in a pot with enough water to cover, boil until tender, drain and cool. Then add to cooled potatoes the following to your liking. For every six servings put in chopped cilantro (1/4 cup), 1 clove of garlic, chopped or mashed, 1 small onion chopped, 1 or 2 thinly sliced peppers (bell peppers or any other mild pepper) and some tarragon (1/2 teaspoon finely ground). Use hands to lightly blend all these ingredients, then add some olive oil (1/4 to 1/3 cup) and enough wine for flavor (a dry red or white wine seems to work best, about ¼ cup). Season with salt or pepper to taste. Serve up cold. NOTE: I have made this salad and in addition to the cilantro I had enough diced celery to add a crunchy texture.

## Scalloped Tomatoes

The humble tomato, intrinsic to the cuisine of the American Southwest, traveled the world from its native lands of Central and South America before it became a popular ingredient in California cooking. Spanish conquistadors discovered the healthful and flavorful benefits of tomatoes on their explorations of the New World, from Mexico and South America tomatoes were collected and taken back to Spain. In Spain, the tomato's use in food was amplified and enhanced, often highlighting it as a major ingredient in recipes. Edible, cooked or raw, and rich in Vitamin C, tomatoes provided flavorful choices in creating a healthy diet.

Original Recipe:

To 1 and ½ cups of tomatoes mix 2 slices of broken bread pieces, 1 stalk finely chopped celery, 1 small onion, chopped, some sugar and salt and pepper. Put all in buttered dish and put in slow over about 1 hour.

Modern version:

Ingredients: 4 to 5 large tomatoes cut into bite-size pieces. 2 cups of breadcrumbs (rye or whole wheat). 1 large celery stalk, diced small. 1 small onion, diced small. 2 Tablespoons white sugar. ½ teaspoon salt. Pepper to taste.

Directions. Use a deep casserole pan. Butter it heavily with cooking margarine or butter. In a large bowl, combine all ingredients EXCEPT tomatoes, stir until thoroughly mixed, then add tomatoes and mix again. Pour into baking dish, bake at 300 degrees on middle rack, until breadcrumbs begin to toast slightly. Stir to redistribute the mixture and continue baking once more until breadcrumbs are toasted on top. Serve warm. A sprinkle of shredded cheese is a wonderful topping for this dish. Note: In this recipe, it is wise to add tomatoes last, to prevent them from breaking down and turning into mush.

## Gold Rush Vegetables

It wasn't just men who came to California seeking gold. California was unique among the western territories in that women could own land and operate a business in their own name. Because of this, women flocked to the golden state to find their own gold and it wasn't the dust and nuggets that men spent long days looking for. Women were among the first pioneering small-business owners. They realized gold by fulfilling the everyday household needs of miners, especially in the field (quite literally) of cooking.

Miners were a hearty lot who, for the most part, were uncomplaining about what they had to eat. However, when given the opportunity to enjoy a home-cooked meal, a miner would offer up a good bit of his gold to the cook. As was the case with Luzena Wilson, who in 1849 cooked her way to prosperity in the mining camps of northern California.

Luzena, with her husband and two sons, made the overland trek to the mining fields of California near Sacramento. The family arrived looking worse for the journey. While her husband Mason tried his luck at gold mining, Luzena set up a campfire kitchen and began cooking for her hungry family. That first campfire meal provided Luzena the opportunity to put some gold in her pocket when a miner caught the aroma of her biscuits and offered Luzena a ten-dollar gold piece for a meal. Luzena gladly sold the dinner and in doing so, opened up business.

In southern California a like story took place with the family of Mary Jane Welty. Mary, her husband, Johnson and a patch of children came west over the treacherous Mojave Desert. They made their way up to the high mountain settlement of Big Bear Valley where a gold strike was in progress. Johnson didn't fare well in Big Bear, but Mary kept food in the stomachs of her family and made money on the side by selling meals to miners. One season in the cold mountains of Big Bear convinced the Weltys to head for lower ground a ways further south. They set down roots in Temecula, a bustling stage stop town that needed the hospitality of a restaurant and lodge. Mary and her daughters opened a 'cook shop' and hotel, which proved to be the best investment the family ever made.

The two recipes included here were typical offerings of mining camp cooks. The first one is most common in that it is a baked bean dinner. The other recipe is for a corn relish that was a sought-after addition to any miner's fare for it added spicy flavor where none existed. Both recipes use common ingredients for the time period and exemplify the culinary creativeness of frontier cooking.

### Gold Rush Bean Dinner

Ingredients: 3 Cups dried navy beans (1 and ½ pound package), ¾ pound salt pork (or sliced bacon), 2 bunches of chopped green onions, ¼ Cup dark brown sugar, 2 teaspoons dry mustard (ground mustard powder), ½ Cup molasses, ¼ Cup tomato ketchup, salt and pepper to taste.

Directions: Wash beans in tepid water, remove all dirt pieces and stones. Put enough water in a big pot to equal twice the amount of beans, cover and let sit in cool spot over night.

Next day, drain off water and put in same amount of fresh water then put pot on to boil over medium fire, once boiling reduce heat to simmer, cover and simmer 30 minutes. Remove from heat, cool a little bit then drain beans, but save the cooking water. To bake beans, put beans in kettle and add the trimmed pork (leave some fat on for flavoring), add all other ingredients, including 1 cup of the cooking water, stir to blend, cover with kettle lid and bake in oven at 300 degrees for up to 6 hours. Stir every hour, add a little more cooking water if beans start to get dry.

## All-Purpose Corn Relish

This relish is used to spice up just about any dish, from scrambled eggs, to pork, to roasted potatoes.

Ingredients: ¾ Cup whole kernel cooked corn (use canned or frozen corn, a good way to use leftover corn), ½ pound of firm tomatoes diced into small chunks, 1/3 cup chopped strong onion (red onions or white 'cooking' onions), 1 Tablespoon of fresh chopped Basil, 1 Tablespoon of olive oil and 2 Teaspoons of red-wine vinegar.

Directions: In a skillet pour olive oil and brown onions until golden and remove to cool in bowl, do not drain oil. Once cooled, add remaining ingredients, toss lightly and put aside in icebox (refrigerate). Serve at room temperature as a topping for entrée or vegetable.

## Loma Linda Entrée Salad

The vegetarian culinary habits of early California pioneers are best exhibited in this salad fit for a dinner entrée recipe hailing from Loma Linda, a Seventh-day Adventist community in the heart of San Bernardino valley. These early vegetarians made delicious use of the valley's rich soil for growing a variety of vegetables and fruit.

Loma Linda, home to the Seventh-day Adventists and the world famous Loma Linda University and Loma Linda University Medical Center had one of the humblest beginnings in all of California.

In the late 1800s a land boom and railroad enterprise made traveling by rail to California cheap and convenient to mid westerners. California-bound visitors came in droves and in doing so spurred the tourist hotel trade. Any spot along the rail line was a good gamble for business operators looking to cash in by building hotels to put up tourists. Throughout the San Bernardino area guest lodges sprang up to the sound of tourist dollars. Some enterprising men decided that Mound City, with its panoramic views of the local mountains and in-between proximity to the twin cities of San Bernardino and Riverside would be the ideal tourist hotel destination. They were wrong.

The Mound City Hotel went bust shortly after opening up for business. All was not lost, in the late 1890s, yet another group of enterprising men opened up the hotel under a different name: The Loma Linda Hotel. The Loma Linda hotel went bust.

Then in 1905, the Seventh-day Adventist church purchased the property, kept the name (after all, it did mean 'pretty hill' in Spanish) and opened a health sanitarium and nursing school. The rest, as the story goes, is history! The legacy of Loma Linda lives on in one of the most successful medical communities in the nation.

Original Recipe from 1928.

What and How: In a large bowl or kettle combine: 1 and ½ cups each of cooked Black beans, Navy beans, Corn niblets; ½ cup each of diced Red bell peppers, Green bell peppers, Red onion, Celery and cooked Carrots; 2 Tablespoons each fresh chopped Basil and fresh Cilantro and 1 thinly diced fresh Jalapeno pepper. Lightly toss all ingredients then add the following: 1 cup Orange juice, 2 Tablespoons Lime juice, ½ cup red vinegar or apple cider vinegar, 1 orange, peeled and segmented into bite-size pieces. Combine all ingredients; stir gently with large spoon to mix. Chill and serve over cold steamed rice or fresh lettuce.

**Crunchy Corned Potatoes**

Put away that frozen convenience bag of potato wedges to heat and serve. Before there were such frozen food items at a grocery store, your could take corn flakes and make your own "cottage fried" baked potatoes.

The California corn flake connection is to the credit of Mr. Will Keith Kellogg of Battle Creek, Michigan. Mr. Kellogg, also known as the cereal king, is responsible for a wide array of boxed cereals, especially corn flakes. Will Kellogg and his brother Dr. John Harvey Kellogg created ready-made cereal by accident one day when they flattened wheat berries into small thin flakes and baked them. The result was breakfast food that was easy to prepare and nutritious. One grain led to another and corn flakes were born. On February 19, 1906, Will Keith Kellogg founded the Battle Creek Toasted Corn Flake Company to mass-produce breakfast cereal to the general public. Kellogg very nearly became a millionaire overnight and could afford to indulge in other passions, such as horses.

Kellogg's love for purebred Arabian horses brought him to the Pomona Valley in southern California. He bought 377 acres of prime horse country to start a breeding program from a herd he purchased in Indio. In later years he added to his collection with horses imported from Egypt, Arabia, England and Poland.

While Californians enjoyed Kellogg's cereals they also got the chance to visit his horse ranch. By 1926, Kellogg was offering public entertainment of horse shows and the shows continue to this day. Come to think of it, Kellogg's corn flake cereal is as popular as ever, too!

Original 19 28 Recipe: To make 16 helpings you'll need: A large roasting pan well greased with vegetable shortening, preheated oven to 350 degrees. Slice 1 and 1/3 pounds of potatoes into ½ inch wedges (to peel or not to peel is your decision). In a shallow bowl have ready 4 eggs, well beaten. In another bowl have ready 3 cups of corn flake crumbs (take a box of corn flake cereal and put flakes in large paper bag, using your palms, smash flakes into crumbs, measure out 3 cups) combined with 2 Tablespoons of garlic salt and 6 Tablespoons of Chili powder. Proceed to dip potato wedges into egg batter then into corn flake crumbs, coat completely and place in greased roasting pan. Proceed until all potato wedges are coated with egg and crumbs. Work quickly. Put in oven on medium rack and bake until browned on top, remove pan, use spatula to turn potatoes and bake again until browned. Serve immediately. Note, depending on your oven and type of potatoes used, it may take as long as 30 minutes on each side to brown and crisp the potatoes.

**Automobile Picnic Salad**

Leave it to a Californian to devise an early tailgate party recipe! The logic fits; after all, the first national automobile association was founded in Los Angeles in 1900. This recipe for an automobile picnic salad is from 1905, a significant road sign on the cultural highway signaling the impact that automobiles had on California society.

What and How: Cut into small pieces four medium-sized tomatoes. Draining off the juice and rejecting it from the salad; two medium-sized heads of torn lettuce or cabbage, four stalks of chopped celery and one-half cup pickled olives. Mix thoroughly and put together with the following dressing: Beat one egg until creamy; pour over it four tablespoons of vinegar, place in double boiler over scalding water, stir constantly until thick. Remove dressing from heat and add the following: one teaspoon butter, stir until melted, then one-half teaspoon each dry mustard and salt, stir in to blend, then add dash of pepper and enough sweet cream to make the dressing the consistency of cream. After adding dressing to salad, top it off with pieces of leftover cooked meat such as chicken or ham. Garnish with red nasturtium blossoms. Place in good size bowl and cover tightly with butcher paper for travel.

**Poetic Salad for a Sunday Gathering**

Californians were no exception to the late-Victorian practice of providing entertaining food in combination with parlor entertainment! As was the practice in the late 1800s, food dishes that provided a topic of conversation were all the rage and nearly every good hostess had at least one poetic recipe. This particular one shows up from time to time with personal liberties taken by the hostess to accommodate her menu. Originally credited (yet to be documented) to the Revered Sidney Smith of St. Paul's Church, London, this recipe is from the files of Miss Broome of Berkeley, California.

Original Recipe from 1900.

Two large potatoes (boiled) passed through a kitchen sieve.
Smoothness and softness to the salad give;
Of mordent mustard add a single spoon,
Distrust the condiment that bites too soon;
But deem it not, thou man of herbs, a fault,
To add a double quantity of salt;
Four time the spoon of oil of Lucca crown,
Add twice with vinegar procured from town;
True flavor needs it, and your poet begs
The pounded yellow of two well-boiled eggs.
Let onion's atoms lurk within the bowl,
And scarce suspected animate the whole;
And, lastly, in the flavor'd compound toss
A magic spoonful of anchovy sauce.
Oh! Great and glorious, and herbaceous treat,
'Twould the dying anchorite to eat;
Back to the world he'd turn his weary soul,
And plunge his fingers in the salad bowl.

# CHAPTER ELEVEN
# SALSAS

**Basic Salsa**

This is the most basic of salsas. All-purpose in nature and ingredients, this traditional recipe leaves ample room for experimentation.

Ingredients:

2 ripe tomatoes peeled and chopped.

1 Serrano pepper seeded and chopped. (However, I usually I do not take out the seeds).

¼ cup chopped fresh cilantro leaves and a few stems.

1 small onion, chopped fine.

I small garlic clove, chopped fine. Salt to taste.

Directions: In a medium bowl combine all prepared ingredients and toss lightly with a spoon or spatula. Store in refrigerator: serve at room temperature. This salsa freezes well.

Makes about 1 and ½ cups, depending on the size of tomatoes.

**Chunky Tomato Salsa**

California's contribution to this recipe is the use of orange juice instead of water.

Ingredients:

3 or 4 large ripe tomatoes equal to 1 pound.

1 small onion; chopped or minced fine.

6 hot peppers of your choice. Chopped fine.

1 clove crushed garlic. Salt to taste.

¼ cup fresh cilantro leaves, no stems.

¼ to ½ cup orange juice.

Directions. In order listed, combine all ingredients, lightly stir to mix, refrigerate for at least 1 hour before serving.


## Cooked Tomatillo Sauce

Ingredients:

1-pound fresh tomatillos.

1 small onion, chopped.

2 Jalapeno peppers, chopped.

1-teaspoon salt and 1-teaspoon sugar.

1-tablespoon olive oil

Fresh cilantro, chopped (optional).

Directions: Remove outer husks from tomatillos and place whole into a saucepan with 4 cups water, bring to a boil on high heat and immediately reduce heat to a simmer. Cook for 10 minutes. Drain and put tomatillos in a blender, allow to cool for a few minutes, and then add all other ingredients, except olive oil. Blend on low until creamy but with light chunky texture. Transfer to a saucepan, add olive oil and simmer on medium heat for 5 minutes. Cool. Taste test; if too bitter or sour, add a little more sugar. Refrigerate. May be frozen.


## Fresh Tomatillo Salsa

Using fresh uncooked tomatillos brings out the zest in this salsa. It is best to use this salsa within a day or two of making.

Ingredients:

1-pound fresh tomatillos (about 10 or 12) remove husks and wash well. Chop fine or process in blender until a chunky purée.

2 or 3 fresh hot peppers, chopped fine.

¼ cup each: chopped green onions and cilantro leaves.

1 teaspoon each of olive oil and sugar.

Salt to taste.

Directions. Place all prepared ingredients in large bowl. Using a handheld potato masher, blend all ingredients as you would to mash potatoes, and then stir lightly with a spoon. As with the cooked salsa recipe, you may care to add more sugar if the taste is too bitter or sour.

## Pico De Gallo

This salsa is perfect over meats or egg and cheese dishes such as a quiche or omelet.

Ingredients:

2 tomatoes, diced

1 small onion, chopped fine.

1 cup of peeled and diced fresh cucumber.

6 hot to mild fresh radishes, diced.

1 stalk of celery, diced fine.

4 hot peppers, chopped fine.

Juice of one medium lime. Salt to taste.

In large bowl combine together all ingredients, saving lime juice for last. Squeeze lime juice over vegetable, sprinkle a little salt and blend with large spoon. Refrigerate. It is best to use this salsa within 5 days.

## Basic Guacamole

Here are a few words of appreciation regarding the alligator pear, better known as avocado. The use and enjoyment of avocado dates back many centuries. In Peru, avocado seeds were discovered buried along with mummies dating back to 750 B.C. And in ancient Mayan Mexico, avocados were a delicacy enjoyed by royalty. The Spanish name for an avocado was *aguacate*, which has been corrupted to avocado. California leads the nation with ninety-five percent of the total number of avocados produced in the U.S. Within that percentage is a southern California lead with a whopping forty-five percent of California's entire crop coming out of San Diego County.

Southern California's commercial avocado farming industry started in the 1920s with the discovery of an unusual avocado tree in La Habra. One fine summer day, postman Rudolf Hass came upon a tree that had taken root in his backyard. Like no other he had seen, the tree bore avocadoes unlike any other in the state. The tree and its fruit were named for its discoverer, and so the story goes about the most popular kind of avocado grown and marketed from California: the Hass Avocado.

Ingredients:

3 or 4 ripe avocados, peeled and pitted, cut into chunks.

1 small onion chopped very fine or minced.

2 Serrano peppers, chopped fine.

1 tablespoon of limejuice.

A few sprigs of fresh cilantro, chopped fine (about 1/8 cup).

Salt to taste.

In medium bowl, place chunks of avocados and mash with fork or potato masher. Add all other ingredients and blend well with fork or spoon. Serve immediately or refrigerate in tightly covered container.


## Mild Guacamole

Ingredients:

2 ripe avocadoes, peeled, pitted and chopped.

1 small tomato, chopped.

½ small onion, chopped fine.

1 Tablespoon of lemon juice.

½ teaspoon each, garlic powder and salt.

Directions: In medium bowl, mash avocados with fork or potato masher. Add all other ingredients and stir with fork to blend. Serve immediately or refrigerate in tightly covered container.

**Spinach and Bread Sauce**

Before the use of flour and butter or flour and water to thicken a sauce, bread was soaked in vinegar or wine to create a paste for thickening. This recipe is of Southern origins that were most likely adapted by former slaves who came to California for freedom's sake. The use of spinach is more common in California, but possibly secondary to using 'greens' of traditional African-American cooking. This recipe is in and of itself a classic example of how California's stand against slavery upon statehood in 1850 contributed to diversity in culture not represented elsewhere in the American West.

This sauce may be served over meat, vegetables or egg dishes.

Ingredients: 1 Cup fresh white bread crumbs (no crust), ¼ cup dry white wine, ½ pound cleaned spinach leaves, 6 cilantro sprigs, 2 sprigs fresh parsley, ½ teaspoon each dried tarragon (ground) and dried sage (ground), 1/8 teaspoon of dry mustard powder, ½ cup heavy cream, salt and pepper.

Directions: In a bowl, drown breadcrumbs (soak) in wine to moisten well. In a skillet over low heat, stir soaked breadcrumb (with wine) until paste forms. (Once heated the breadcrumbs will "melt" and form a paste with the wine it absorbed). Remove from heat to cool. In a blender, put remainder of ingredients (EXCEPT for cream, salt and pepper) and slowly add the warmed bread/wine paste to blender. Blend for one minute until mixture is smooth and transfer it back to skillet. Add cream; stir to blend under medium heat. Remove and add salt and pepper to taste. Note: It is best to tear or cut all greenery into small pieces in preparation for blending. After washing greenery, let drain on paper towel to prevent adding water to sauce.

**Pesto**

Basil is one of America's best-loved herbs. Originally from India, Basil is most closely associated with Greco-Roman cooking. In California's numerous Little Italy neighborhoods, it is basil's irresistible aroma that attracts one's appetite. According to Italian custom, basil is also known as the "Kiss-me-Nicholas" seasoning. No wonder it is so popular in cooking! Not only does basil add delectable flavor—it promotes romance!

This 1920's recipe is one of the easiest pesto recipes I have come across. Be sure to use the best olive oil your pocket book will allow. This recipe calls for using a mortar and pestle, an antique form of grinding and blending rarely employed by today's household cook. Utilizing a blender makes quick and efficient work in place of a mortar and pestle.

Pound in a mortar 2 cups fresh Basil leaves with 3 minced Garlic cloves and ½ cup of Pine nuts. Transfer to large deep bowl (or leave in blender) and stir in 1-Cup Virgin Olive oil, then work in 1-Cup fresh grated Parmesan cheese. Blend until pesto is same consistency of heavy cream. 1 and ½ cups pesto.

If you desire a thinner pesto, add a little more olive oil. Use this pesto has a dip for croutons, bread or vegetables or as a pasta topping. Romano cheese may be used instead of Parmesan. For spicy addition, try grinding in a few peppercorns at the beginning of the recipe. Pesto makes a great sandwich spread in place of mayonnaise.

**Italian Salsa Verde**

Spicy, but not peppery hot in comparison to traditional Mexican salsa verde, this Italian green sauce was created to use cold as a salad dressing or as a meat-dipping sauce served on the side. Substituting the parsley with cilantro will yield a more modern California-styled verde sauce.

Original 1920's recipe: In a large bowl, combine 1 cup of minced parsley with 1 clove minced garlic, 2 Tablespoons of minced green onions, 1 teaspoon salt and 2 cups olive oil. Beat with whisk (Or use blender) until smooth. Stir in a little lemon juice until thinned to desired consistency (Add up to ½ cup lemon juice, blend in a little at a time). About 3 cups. Improves when refrigerated overnight.

**Aztec Mole (mo-lay)**

If a sauce could be considered sacred to a culture, it is mole. To read about the history of mole, refer to the recipe in the <u>Meats</u> section of this book: <u>Mole De Guajolote (Turkey in Mole Sauce)</u>. The aforementioned recipe is an example of a traditional mole laden with numerous ingredients. If you desire a quick way to make mole, the following 1920's recipe is ideal.

Directions: In a saucepan combine the following: 15 ounces Tomato sauce, 4 ounces Picante-style hot sauce, 4 Tablespoons unsweetened Cocoa powder, 1 teaspoon each, ground Cumin & Oregano, ½ teaspoon Garlic salt, dash each of ground Cloves, Nutmeg and Ginger. Bring to boil on medium heat, stir constantly to prevent scorching. Boil one minute then reduce to simmer for 15 minutes. Makes little over 2 cups. Recipe may be doubled. This sauce freezes nicely and is a convenient way to always have mole on hand for spicing up leftover meats or using with egg dishes.


**Gold Rush Tomato Ketchup**

Ketchup, "catsup" and "catchup" have been in use for centuries. The name, in whatever form you care to use, identifies a sauce named for a Chinese pickled fish sauce. In the beginning, America's favorite ketchup was not made from tomatoes. The most popular varieties of ketchup were made from walnuts, cranberries or raisins. Recipes for cranberry catchup were popular in Colonial homes and American Indians taught settlers how to make catsups from a variety of nuts, especially walnuts.

Today, ketchup is synonymous with the restaurant styled tomato product so beloved by diners to pour over hamburgers and fried potatoes. Canned and bottled tomato ketchups have been in use since the mid-1800s, at which time they were used as much as an ingredient in recipes as they were for table condiments. Ever popular with California's gold rushers, just about every mining camp cook, from 1849 on, had his own recipe for making tomato ketchup. For a recipe that uses ketchup to flavor a typical gold rush dinner, flip to the <u>Vegetables and Rice</u> section of this book and look for the recipe: <u>Gold Rush Beans</u>.

Original Recipe: 1/8 bushel firm and ripe tomatoes (about 6 and ½ pounds), 1 large sweet onion, ¼ pound of dark brown sugar, 3 Tablespoons allspice, 1 teaspoon cayenne pepper and 1 quart apple cider vinegar. Put into big dutch oven (large canning kettle), chopped tomatoes into eighths (no need to peel), chopped real fine the onion, add all other ingredients except vinegar. Over indirect fire (medium heat) bring mixture to boil real hard. Stir like crazy for several minutes. Remove from fire and stir in vinegar, then put back on fire and simmer for a couple hours, stir often. (Simmer on low heat for 2 hours. It helps to use a potato masher to stir and mash ketchup and it simmers). The type of tomatoes used for this recipe decides the flavor. Also, this recipe takes some personalizing. Therefore, just before the last two hours of simmering, take a tablespoon of ketchup out for tasting at which point you may want to add additional sugar (for a sweeter taste) or salt for a tangy flavor.

# CHAPTER TWELVE
# BREADS and DESERTS

## Cheese Biscuits

Because of the addition of cheese in this recipe, these biscuits brown very quickly, so keep an eye on the oven. To cut in butter to the flour mixture, use an electric mixer on medium speed. However, if you have the inkling to do right by this recipe then use a long tined fork and cut the butter into the flour by making quick, firm pressing marks using the flat bottom side of the tined end. Working the fork in a crisscross pattern will cut the butter into the flour, rendering an even distribution of a crumbly mixture.

Original Recipe:

To 1 cup of sifted flour in mixing bowl (I use all-purpose flour and I never sift it), add ¼ teaspoon salt, stir and cut in 1/3 cup of soft butter or well-set bacon fat (butter is preferred to bacon fat, some margarines work as well). Cut until mixture resembles pea-sized crumbs throughout. Then work in 1 cup grated hard cheese (extra sharp cheddar is especially tasty), if dough is too stiff, add a little buttermilk (in my experience the dough has never been too stiff, the type of fat used makes the difference). Use hands to work into a ball, and then pat out on floured surface so dough is about 1 inch thick (or roll with bottle or pastry pin) and with small closed-ended cutter (a small straight sided jar or can) cut down into dough without twisting. (The trick is not to twist the cutter, instead, firmly press cutter into dough in one firm downward stroke. This action results is a soft "puff" sound. Tap on the end of the cutter to release biscuit). Bake on pan bottom (cookie sheet, lightly greased with shortening) in hot oven (preheated, 375 degrees) until light brown on top. Watch carefully, these biscuits burn quickly.

## Cornbread Sticks

Maybe in your wanderings through antiques stores, flea markets or thrift shops you have seen a heavy cast iron pan divided into several compartments shaped like a cob of corn? If so, buy, beg or borrow one of those pans… You now have an authentic recipe for a corn stick pan! These should be served fresh out of the oven, hot and crispy. Don't try to split a corn stick to butter it, just lather the butter on top and leave be or serve with your favorite pancake syrup. As with other authentic recipes I have listed, the only modern adaptations needed are in parenthesis.

In batter bowl, beat together 3 Cups of Meal (packaged yellow corn meal), 3 Cups of Milk (whole milk or buttermilk), 2 Eggs, 2 Tablespoons of melted Lard (shortening), 1 and ½ Teaspoons of Salt and 1 Tablespoon of Baking Powder. Bake in heavily greased Bread-Stick Pans in hot Oven (400 degrees, preheated, center rack) until browned and crisp (about 20 minutes).

## Stagecoach Wheels (Buns)

This is a fanciful sweetened version of commonplace bread buns. These yeast sweet buns are ideal for a special brunch or to serve in place of coffeecake.

Original Recipe:

Over medium heat in a small saucepan bring 1 cup of milk to boil, remove from heat and stir in a half cup sugar, 4 heavy pats butter (4 ounces or half a cube), 2 teaspoonfuls of salt. Stir all this and leave until luke warm to the touch. Transfer this to very large mixing bowl and add 2 yeast cakes, which were dissolved in warm water (Use 2 small packets of bread yeast—available in grocery stores—follow package directions for dissolving), next in a small bowl beat 3 whole eggs until creamy (no need to break out the electric mixer, use a large spoon or whisk). Slowly add eggs to liquid, stir well to blend then add 4 or more cups of flour, one cup at a time (at the most, it make take 4 ½ cups flour, dough should be soft and a little sticky, so coat your hands with a baking spray or butter before handling dough). Next, knead dough softly (handle lightly, do not overwork the dough or the buns will be tough) on hard floured surface. Let dough rest until doubled (Put dough into a greased bowl that is 2 x size of dough ball, cover bowl with tea towel, let rise out of a drafty area until doubled, inside a cupboard is a good area. When dough has doubled, punch down and knead again and roll out on greased cookie sheet so dough is flat and near in size to cookie sheet.

To sweeten and spice the buns, butter the slab of dough and heavily sprinkle brown sugar, cinnamon, then roll long-ways as though rolling up a rug. Use a wide sharp knife to slice the roll into buns (Make 1 inch slices, a serrated knife works well for this task, if the knife sticks, spray with an baking spray). Place stagecoach wheels on buttered cookie sheet; all friendly like (it's okay if they touch) let them rise and then bake in oven (350 degrees, on center rack) until lightly brown.

### Coricios (Corn Cookies)

By now you may have noticed that corn meal was a staple for baking in pioneer recipes. These corn cookies are surprisingly good—not what you might expect from yet another corn meal recipe.

Ingredients:

2 Cups of maseca—finely ground corn flour.

1 Cup yellow corn meal.

1 Tablespoon baking powder.

1 Teaspoon salt.

1 Cup sugar.

1 Teaspoon vanilla extract.

Dash ground nutmeg (no more than ½ teaspoon).

1 cup shortening or margarine.

3 eggs, beaten.

Some milk (not likely to need more than a half cup)

Directions. Preheat oven to 350 degrees, if your oven runs hot, reduce to 325 degrees. Lightly grease a cookie sheet. In large mixing bowl,
combine all dry ingredients and stir to blend. Melt shortening in separate pan and set aside (just barely melt it). Take beaten eggs and cooled
shortening and add to dry ingredients, stir well with spoon (or electric
mixer), dough should be stiff, but if too hard to handle, add milk until
dough can be formed in your hands like clay. Make shaped cookies by
rolling and forming dough with your hands. Form circles, hearts or tri-
angle shapes, place on cookie sheet and bake in oven until solid to the
touch. Don't judge if they are done by appearance, touch them to be
sure. Store in airtight container. Serve with milk or for a more authentic
treat, serve these cookies with Mexican Hot Chocolate (see recipe).


**Petticoat Cookies**

These are the most basic of shortbread cookies. Do not let the sim-
plicity of the few ingredients fool you and *never* substitute margarine or
any other butter substitute for the butter called for in this recipe.

Original Recipe:

Sift together several times 5 Cups Flour with 1 Cup fine Powdered
Sugar. (Use a large mixing bowl and an electric mixer on low speed to do
the "sifting" for about 1 minute). Then Cut in 2 Cups of soft Butter (use
softened table butter, equal to 4 cubes, blend with mixer). Dough will be
stiff and warm. Shape it between your hands (knead lightly), turn dough
into long roll (a cookie log) and chill in icebox overnight (Chill in refrigerator 3 or more hours, no need to let it chill overnight unless you want
to). Place roll on floured board (or wax paper) and slice thin (1/2 inch).
Bake on cookie sheet until very lightly brown in slow oven (about 20
minutes at 325 degrees, preheated). Do not grease the cookie sheet; I

advise using baking parchment to prevent these cookies from getting too brown.


## Mexican Wedding Cookies

As with many of the recipes throughout this book, this one is directly descended from California's Mexican heritage and culture. These wedding cookies are a delicious example of a typical Mexican recipe that became popular with all Californians. Traditionally, these cookies were served only at weddings. Now, of course, they are readily available in supermarkets and specialty stores and are welcome treats on any occasion. The melt-in-your-mouth sweetness of these delicate cookies is in actuality, an easy recipe to master. Please notice the absence of eggs in this recipe.

Original Recipe:

Take a large mixing bowl and a heavy long-handled wooden spoon to 1-cup fresh soft butter and whip with spoon until fluffy. To this beat in 1 cup powdered sugar, 2 teaspoons water, small amount of crushed vanilla bean and a handful of toasted pecan pieces. Then stir in a little pinch of cinnamon and 2 cups flour. Use fingers to shape dough into spoon-sized balls. Bake in medium oven on ungreased sheet until cookies are lightly browned on bottom. Cool them on tea towels or flour sack. When cooled, roll cookies one at a time in flour sack of powdered sugar. Repeat to double coat each cookie.

Modern Version:

Ingredients:

1-cup sweet butter (2 cubes). This is unsalted butter and is available in stores. Leave butter out to soften to room temperature.

2 cups powdered sugar. Use 1 cup in the recipe and 1 cup to coat the cookies after baking.

2 teaspoon of tepid water.

1 teaspoon vanilla extract.

¼ teaspoon ground cinnamon.

2 cups all-purpose flour.

Directions. Use a large mixing bowl and electric beater or, if you have the arm power, a strong long-handled whisk to beat the batter by hand. Preheat oven to 325 degrees. Do not grease cookie sheet. For cooling, it is best to use either a wire rack or paper towels.

Put softened butter, water, sugar, vanilla and cinnamon in large mixing bowl and beat on high for 2 minutes. Batter will be fluffy. Add flour one cup at a time and mix on low, 1 minute for each cup. Dough will be stiff, but manageable. Use hands to shape cookies into 1-inch balls. Place on cookie sheet and bake in preheated oven on center rack. Bake about 20 minutes. Watch carefully, these cookies should not brown on top before browning on bottom. Only the bottoms should appear lightly browned. Remove cookies with spatula (they are delicate at this stage and will break easily) to cool on rack or paper towels. After baking and cooling all cookies, put the extra cup of powdered sugar into a small paper bag (lunch sized brown bags are ideal for this next step) and place 2 or 3 cookies at a time into the bag and then gently roll them around to coat with sugar. For double-coated cookies, repeat the "sugar-bag" process. Store cookies in an airtight container.

### Honey-Cake Bars

In the 1800s, California's citrus industry was a statewide field of dreams for beekeepers and honey packagers. Any flavor variety of honey works well for this recipe. However, to make it authentic, try using orange-blossom honey.

Preheat oven to 375 degrees. Butter a loaf pan (9x13 inches). In large bowl beat 3 large eggs until creamy. (Throughout this recipe you can beat by hand using a large heavy spoon or use an electric hand mixer). Next, stir in 1/3 cup softened table butter with 1-cup honey and nutmeats of your choice (3/4 cup chopped walnut pieces). Stir hard to blend well and then add 2 teaspoons of baking powder, ½ teaspoon each of baking soda and table salt and 1-teaspoon ground cinnamon or nutmeg or ginger. Stir again to blend and then add 3-½ cups sifted flour (cake flour), 1 cup at a time, mixing well after each cup. Spoon batter into baking pan and bake on center rack about 30 minutes or until the center springs back when lightly touched with fingertip. Cool completely before cutting into bars.

## Irish Potato Pudding with Sweet Sugar Sauce

To be sure… if I were not descended from the Irish clans of Mac Egan, Mac Morgan, (Mc) Corley, and Wright… I would not believe there could be a dessert recipe such as this! Going all the way back to Virginia of 1632, this recipe went "Out West" with my Corley cousins.

Original Recipe:

To two and ½ pound potatoes, mashed well, add ½ pound of sugar, ½ pound of butter, and 4 large eggs with whites. Beat this all together. For flavor add orange or lemon peel and a large glass of wine. Bake in oven to set. Serve warm with Sweet Sugar Sauce (follows after modern version of this recipe).

Modern Version:

Ingredients: 2½ pounds of peeled and cooked Idaho Gold or Yukon Gold baking potatoes (bake, and then peel. Good way to use extra baked potatoes). Mash or whip potatoes thoroughly.

1-cup white table sugar.

1 cup softened butter.

4 whole large eggs.

1 teaspoon each, orange extract, vanilla extract.

6 ounces of red wine (another variation is to use orange juice.)

Directions. Preheat oven to 350 degrees and butter a 2 quart-size or larger, casserole-baking pan (use butter, margarine or a baking oil spray) that has a lid.

In a large mixing bowl mash potatoes then beat in the butter and sugar. Next, add eggs one at a time, blending well after each. Then add all remaining ingredients, in the order listed. Transfer to baking dish and bake in oven's center rack, covered, 25 minutes.

Cool slightly and serve warm in individual bowls, top with Sweet Sugar Sauce.

### Sweet Sugar Sauce

Original Recipe:

Over slow flame, in pot, stir wine, sugar and butter to taste. If using table butter, skim off salt as it rises. Stir to warm and serve over pudding.

Modern Version:

In a medium saucepan, over medium heat, stir 1 cup of sweet butter (available at grocery stores in dairy section) until melted, then add 1 cup of white sugar and ½ cup of orange juice or red wine, stir until all sugar is dissolved, about 3minutes. Turn up heat to highest temperature and stir constantly for 2 minutes. Mixture will begin to break a boil. Remove from heat, cool slightly then serve warm over pudding. This sauce can be re-warmed in a microwave oven on low temperature.


### No-Egg Chocolate Cake

We are quite accustomed to making cakes, from scratch or from a mix, with the all-critical addition of eggs. But what if eggs were not available? The hearty pioneers who trekked overland to get to California often made do without the simplest of supplies taken for granted by settlers already here.

Case in point is this summary of a supply list issued by a wagon master in St. Joseph, Missouri to the California-bound pioneers: *2 hundred pounds of flour per each person over 10 years old. 15 pounds each of coffee and sugar per person. 100 pounds bacon for each person over 10 years old. For each wagon's mess (cooking supplies) take 50 pounds each of salt, rice, and dried fruit such as apples and peaches. Each mess should also have 5 bushels of corn meal for cooking and first aid (corn meal was used on sores and sunburned skin). See wagon master for list of general dry good supplies and weaponry.*

Did you notice that chickens are not on the list? It is with good reason that wagon masters did not want the pioneers toting chicken coops along for the ride. Chickens were noisy, smelly and drew the attention of predators such as bears, cougars and coyotes. There was enough hardship to contend without inviting the misery of predators into camp. Hence, the pioneer cook on the trek to California learned quick enough to make-do without an egg to bake with. The next two recipes exemplify the creativeness of wagon train cookery.

Original Recipe.

To make cake without eggs... Sift together 1 Cup Sugar, 1 and ½ Cups Flour, 1/3 Cup Cocoa Powder, 1 teaspoon each Baking Soda and Baking Powder and ½ Teaspoon Salt. Make 2 wells in this. In First well add ½ Cup of Cooking Oil or softened Fat along with 2 Tablespoons of drinking Vinegar (White Vinegar). In Second well put 1 Cup Water. Stir quickly and put right away into a greased pan to bake in hot Dutch Oven until center is raised and firm.

## No-Egg Shoo-Fly Pie

Original Recipe. For one family-sized pie use a 9-inch pan, fit it to your liking (Meaning, use your own pie pastry recipe.) In a large bowl mix together these ingredients in order presented. Use 3/4 Cup boiled Water, cooled to luke warm and add to it ¾ Cup Molasses spiced with ¼ Teaspoon each of Nutmeg, Ginger, Cloves, Cinnamon and Salt. Stir well and add ¼ Teaspoon baking Soda. Quickly pour this into prepared pie pan and bake in preheated hot oven (450 degrees) or in large Dutch Oven with pie pan setting on a layer of rocks. (Pioneer cooks often raised the level of a Dutch Oven's baking surface with a layer of rocks... this would be the equivalent of baking this pie on the center rack in a modern oven).

## Walnut Pies

When Spanish Franciscan monks founded missions along the California coast, they spent a great amount time and effort cultivating food-bearing plants. Much to their credit, just outside the greater Los Angeles area is the San Gabriel Mission, where walnut trees, imported by the monks from Spain, were planted and cultivated with enormous success. Today, in this area is the city of Walnut.

In time, as land grants were issued and spread out over California's coasts and inland valleys, walnut groves flourished. In 1867, horticulturist Joseph Sexton established California's fist commercial walnut enterprise. Sexton planted a small grove of English walnut trees in Goleta, Santa Barbara County. By the end of the decade, sixty-five percent of all fertile land in the region of Goleta was successfully being used to harvest English walnuts.

In the 1930s, climate and agricultural studies determined that the valley rich soil of Stockton produced the largest and best walnuts. Today, California's walnut growers have settled in this same central area and in doing so have earned the region the nickname of Walnut Capital of California. Not surprisingly, California produces ninety-nine percent of the commercial walnut supply for the United States.

The following walnut pie recipes date to 1910 and were made possible by using corn syrup. In 1902, the Corn Products Company of New Jersey commercially produced a bottled corn syrup under the brand name: Karo.

## PIE RECIPE # 1: GINGER-WALNUT PIE

Yields: a 9-inch pie. Glass pie plate is recommended: Use your own pie pastry recipe or follow the PAT-A-PIE PASTRY recipe that follows. Oven: Preheated to 350 degrees. Prepare pie pastry and line plate, set aside in cool location (refrigerate) until ready to fill.

Make pie filling as follows: In a large bowl beat together 3 large whole eggs with ½ cup light brown sugar, 1 teaspoon ground ginger, 1 cup of light corn syrup, 3 Tablespoons melted margarine (allow to cool before adding) and 1/8 teaspoon of salt. Beat well so all ingredients are blended, set aside. Then in a separate bowl have 1 and ¼ cup of walnuts pieces (small pieces work best), over the walnuts sprinkle 1 and ½ Tablespoons flour, stir lightly so walnuts are coated with flour, now add walnuts and any flour remaining with the walnuts to the bowl of egg-sugar mixture. Stir well, then pour into prepared pie shell and bake in oven on medium-low rack. Baking time varies depending on heat source. Pie will take about 75 minutes and will be done when it is set in center and shows cracks on top of surface. Cool pie on rack. Serve at room temperature or better to chill it. Note: Pie will appear rounded and puffy, as it cools, the surface shrinks down to the same size as when it was first poured into pie shell. If you use a glass pie plate, the bottom crust will be golden brown when pie is done. As with a pecan pie, it is best to wait until pie is completely cooled before eating.

### PIE RECIPE # 2: CHOCOLATE-WALNUT PIE

The ingredients are slightly different, but the directions are the same as for the above-mentioned recipe.

Ingredients: 3 large eggs, ½ cup light brown sugar, 1 cup light corn syrup, 1/8 teaspoon salt, 1/3 cup melted margarine, 1/3 cup unsweetened cocoa. 1 and ¼ cup of walnut pieces and 1 and ½ Tablespoons flour.

### PAT-A-PIE-PASTRY

This recipe uses oil instead of shortening, lard or butter. Benefits of oil pastry include using heart-healthy oils such as Olive, Soy or Canola. For most people oils are easier to digest than shortenings or butter. For savory entrée pies such as Quiche or Shepherds Pie, try using Olive oil or oils infused with natural flavors from garlic or herbs.

You will not need a rolling pin or mat. Glass pie pans should be used to acquire the appropriate crispness. Metal pans or pottery pans will not render the same texture and flavor as a glass pan.

The following recipe is for one 12-inch pastry shell bottom. For the 9-inch pastry required for the walnut pie recipes and for most dessert pies, make the full pastry recipe, dived dough in half, then divide each half once again. For a 9-inch pie, use three quarters of the dough. Dough may be frozen and thawed for later use.

Ingredients:

2 cups <u>all-purpose</u> flour (do not use self-rising flour, or flours made especially for cake or bread baking)

1 & ½ teaspoons salt (for a dessert pastry use regular table salt. For an entrée pastry try using a seasoned salt or celery salt)

½ cup oil (for a dessert pie use canola oil)

5 tablespoons of ice cold water.

Directions:

1.In a large bowl, use a spoon to lightly mix together all the flour and salt.

2.Measure oil and add the cold water to the oil.

3.Make a well in the flour/salt mixture and pour in the oil/water. Using an electric mixer beat on high (about a minute) until the dough clumps together. You will be able to take a small amount of dough and form a ball. In dry weather it may be necessary to add a bit more water to the dough if it is too dry to form a ball.

4.Place all of the dough (it will be crumbly) into the glass pie pan. Using your fingers, begin to pat the dough in the center. Pat firmly as you work your way out to the sides of the pan and up the to the rim. Crimp or pat down crust rim as you normally do in making a pie. (This dough is very forgiving, if you don't get the results you desire, put the dough back in the bowl, lightly mix it to make it crumbly again, check to see if you might need a little bit more oil or water and start again).

5.The pastry is now ready to fill or bake "blind" if you need to fill the pie after the pastry is baked, in which case, lightly prick holes in the pastry before baking.

6.Keep in mind that this recipe makes a thick crust and it will most likely be necessary to bake it close to the bottom in order to make sure the crust thoroughly browns. It is necessary to cool a dessert pie completely at room temperature *before* refrigeration. Use a rack to cool the pie on, so air can circulate under and around the pie. If the pie is refrigerated before cooling, the crust will become soggy.

**Mexican Flan**

This is a baked classic Mexican dessert often served at holiday meals. Yet at the same time, this flan is simple enough to serve with any dinner. The flan is delicately flavored with vanilla and almond, the perfect finish to any meal.

This original recipe requires a single Mexican flan pan or 8 individual baking cups (6 ounces each). If a flan pan (4-cup size) is not available, using a quiche pan or large and deep pie pan will suffice. This flan is baked in a water bath.

Ingredients:

½ Cup white sugar

1 can sweetened condensed milk

1 Cup whole milk

3 whole Eggs

3 Egg yokes

½ teaspoon each, Vanilla Extract and Almond Extract.

Directions: Put sugar in a small saucepan and heat over medium heat while stirring until sugar browns to a caramel colored liquid. Remove at once and pour into the bottom of flan pan or individual baking cups. Turn flan pan/baking cups to coat the bottoms with caramelized sugar liquid. Do this quickly because the sugar cools and sets quickly. Set aside to allow sugar caramel to harden while you prepare the flan filling.

Heat oven to 325 degrees. In a large bowl combine all remaining ingredients and beat at high speed until thoroughly mixed. Pour filling into flan pan/baking cups. Have a larger pan that the flan pan/baking cups will fit into (a large roasting pan) filled ½ inch with water. Into this water bath, place the filled flan pan/baking cups and set on medium oven rack to bake. Bake 1 hour, until set (will be firm in center). Remove flan from water bath and allow to cool at room temperature, then transfer to refrigerator to cool completely. To serve: cover top of flan with a serving plate (saucer for individual cups), hold plate and flan together and turn upside down to invert flan. Lift off pan, caramel will drip down the molded flan as a sauce. Serve.

**Dated Desserts**

The history of date growing in California is a story of exploration, world travel and enterprise. On February 25, 1776, Father Francisco Garces' trek through the lower desert of southern California found him travelling "three leagues north-north-west across a tiring stretch of sand" in what is now the Coachella Valley, Date Capital of the Americas. Coachella Valley's date farming took root one hundred and twenty-five years after the padre crossed its scorching sand.

In 1901, German native Bernard G. Johnson entered into the valley fresh from a well-digging job. Johnson had acquired learned and practical knowledge of date culture from his extensive travels through Europe and North Africa. His keen enterprising mind saw the Coachella Valley as the right place to start a date colony in the Promised Land of California.

From Algiers, Johnson imported 129 young date palms and laid them down to root in 1903. His first plantings were successful beyond his dreams, so he expanded his dreams by adding subsequent plantings imported from Algiers. Johnson's efforts stirred up a buzz among spectators and the result was a crowd of curious investors showing up in Coachella Valley to buy acreage. Land companies formed, acreage was subdivided and roads were built to crisscross the desert and transform Coachella Valley into an oasis of date-farming commerce. Johnson's visionary dream-come-true is today the largest date harvesting center in the nation. To taste test the richness of Johnson's dream, try one of these delicious date desserts.

## DECADENT DATE COMPOTE

This recipe from 1908 hails from the Coachella Valley and is, perhaps, one of the earliest recipes to put Johnson's dates to culinary use.

How and What: To 1 pound of stoned dates (pitted), cut into quarters and add 1 cup white sugar and 2 cups water. In a double boiler, put water and sugar over medium heat, stir constantly and bring to boil for 1 minute, reduce heat and cook 3 minutes, remove from heat, stir in dates.

Take leave from heat and set next to stove, where warm, but not under fire. Leave set and covered for 1 hour. Next, add ½ cup finely chopped walnuts or pecans, 1/2 teaspoon of vanilla extract and 2 ounces of mellow sherry. Blend well with spoon; put in bowl, chill. Spoon date compote into individual small bowls and top with heavy whipped cream.

## SPICED DATE TEACAKE

Ingredients: Cake: 2 Cups sifted flour, 1 Tablespoon double-acting baking powder, ½ teaspoon salt, 1/2 cup vegetable shortening, ½ cup light brown sugar, 1 and ¼ teaspoons Allspice, 2 large whole eggs, 1 Cup diced pitted dates and ¾ cup whole milk. Topping: 3 Tablespoons white sugar, 1 Tablespoon of grated orange rind, 1 teaspoon grated lemon rind and ¼ cup finely chopped walnuts.

Directions: Stir together flour, baking powder and salt. In separate, larger bowl blend together shortening, brown sugar and Allspice then add to this the eggs and beat well. To the egg/sugar mixture add flour mixture alternately with milk. Pour batter into a 9-inch well-greased cake pan. Mix together the topping ingredients and sprinkle over top of cake batter. Bake in a preheated 350-degree oven for about 40 minutes. Remove to cool on counter for 20 minutes, serve warm from pan.

## DATE SAUCE FOR ICE CREAM

This sauce transforms plain ice cream into a premier dessert. The recipes doubles nicely and freezes well. It can be thawed in a microwave oven on low temperature.

What and How: In a saucepan combine 1 cup water, ½ cup sugar, 1 Tablespoon cornstarch and 1/8 teaspoon salt. Stir over low heat until blended then add 2 Tablespoons of fresh lemon juice (juice from a concentrate will do). Continue to stir and cook until thickened and sauce begins to appear transparent. Then add ¼ cup chopped pitted dates, ¼ cups finely chopped pecans and 1 Tablespoon butter or margarine. Stir to blend, remove from heat and cool. Serve warm over ice cream.

**Sunday Best Scriptural Cake**

In the 1920s, if you mixed old time religion with a little bit of Holly-wood glitz, what did you get? The result is a California-styled evangelism that began with Aimee Semple McPherson, the founder of the Angelus Temple, home to the Church of Foursquare Gospel. Sister Aimee preached a Bible Belt ministry aided by glamorous props on Hollywood stages big enough for the most popular entertainers of the time. One such entertainer was Will Rogers who candidly remarked about California's exceptional growth that "The chambers of commerce take the credit, but we all know that if you'd take away the climate, the scandals, and Aimee we'd have nothing left."

Sister Aimee's brand of religion struck a chord in the communities she attended to and that chord sounded forth a revival in fundamental-ism throughout the state. The menus of Aimee's era echoed this senti-ment. Back in vogue were desserts topped with angle flaked coconut and scripture cakes—a phenomenon that evolved from colonial reli-gious fervor and dedication for integrating the gospel into ordinary ev-eryday activities. The recipe is based on passages from the Bible. As to which version or interpretation of the Bible best suits this recipe... well, this is a matter of religious choice. I have tasted cakes made from this recipe and each one was delicious, however I've never attempted to make the recipe myself. This particular recipe hails from Prospect Park, Cali-fornia in 1919, the same year Sister Aimee made her home in Los Ange-les.

1919 Recipe:

4 and ½ cups of I Kings, iv: 22.

1 cup of Judges, v: 25; last clause.

2 cups of Jeremiah, vi: 20.

2 cups of I Samuel, xxx: 12.

2 cups of Nahum, iii: 12.

2 cups of Numbers, xvii: 8.

Three tablespoons of I Samuel, xiv: 25.

A pinch of Leviticus, ii: 13.

6 Jeremiah, xvii: 11.

Half cup of Judges, iv: 19; last clause.

2 teaspoons of Amos, iv: 5.

Season to taste if II Chronicles, ix: 9.

In a large bowl, blend together I Kings through Jeremiah, vi: 20. Next add in the rest of ingredients to and including a pinch of Leviticus, mix well. Then add remaining ingredients and mix thoroughly. Bake at 325 degrees in a large, well-greased sheet-cake pan until center springs back lightly when touched.

# BIBLIOGRAPHY

Armitage, Susan and Elizabeth James. <u>The Women's West</u>. 1987.

Baver, Helen. <u>California Mission Days</u>. 1951.

Bolton, H. E. and E.D. Adams. <u>California's Story</u>. 1922.

Botkin, B. A. <u>A Treasury of Western Folklore</u>. 1951.

Brown, John Jr., Boyd James. <u>History of San Bernardino and Riverside Counties</u>. 1922

Coit, J. Eliot. <u>Citrus Fruits</u>. 1930.

Coolidge, Dane. <u>Old California Cowboys</u>. 1939.

Cox, Elizabeth. <u>Southern California Miscellany</u>. 2004.

Dunke, Glenn. <u>The Boom Period of the Eighties</u>. 1945.

Emrich, Duncan. <u>It's an Old West Custom</u>. 1949.

Fitzgerald, Bishop, O. P. <u>California Sketches</u>. 1908.

Haten, Leroy and Annie. <u>The Old Spanish Trail</u>. 1954.

<u>Women in the Life of Southern California</u>. Historical Society of Southern California. 1996.

Hutchinson, W. H. <u>California</u>. 1969.

Karolevitz, Robert F. <u>Doctors of the Old West</u>. 1957.

Knowles, Thomas W. <u>The West That Was</u>. 1993.

Lauber, Patricia. <u>Cowboys and Cattle Ranching, Yesterday and Today</u>. 1973.

Leadabrand, Russ. <u>Exploring California's Byways</u>. 1967.

Leadabrand, Russ. <u>Guidebook to California Folklore</u>. 1972.

MacCurdy, Rahne Mable. History of California Fruit Growers Exchange. 1925.

Murphy, Bill. A Pictorial History of California. 1958.

Nelson, Edith Deu Pree. The California Dons. 1962.

Nordhoff, Charles. California for Health, Pleasure and Residence. 1874.

O'Neal, Bill. Best of the West. 1997.

Reece, Daphne. Historic Houses of California. 1983.

Rolle, Charles and John S. Gaines. The Golden State. 1979.

Rush, Philip S. Some Old Ranchos and Adobes. 1965.

Utley, Robert. Encyclopedia of the American West. 1997.

Ward, Geoffrey C. The West. 1996.

White, Stewart Edward. Old California. 1937.

Printed in the United States
35215LVS00004B/52